Boycott!

AMERICAN STUDIES NOW:
CRITICAL HISTORIES OF THE PRESENT

Edited by Lisa Duggan and Curtis Marez

Much of the most exciting contemporary work in American Studies refuses the distinction between politics and culture, focusing on historical cultures of power and protest on the one hand, or the political meanings and consequences of cultural practices, on the other. *American Studies Now* offers concise, accessible, authoritative, e-first books on significant political debates, personalities, and popular cultural phenomena quickly, while such teachable moments are at the forefront of public consciousness.

Boycott!

The Academy and Justice for Palestine

Sunaina Maira

UNIVERSITY OF CALIFORNIA PRESS

University of California Press, one of the most distinguished university presses in the United States, enriches lives around the world by advancing scholarship in the humanities, social sciences, and natural sciences. Its activities are supported by the UC Press Foundation and by philanthropic contributions from individuals and institutions. For more information, visit www.ucpress.edu.

University of California Press
Oakland, California

Library of Congress Cataloging-in-Publication Data

Names: Maira, Sunaina, 1969– author.
Title: Boycott! : the academy and justice for Palestine / Sunaina Maira.
Description: Oakland, California : University of California Press, [2018] | Includes bibliographical references. |
Identifiers: LCCN 2017030344 (print) | LCCN 2017037257 (ebook) | ISBN 9780520967854 (epub) | ISBN 9780520294882 (cloth : alk. paper) | ISBN 9780520294899 (pbk. : alk. paper)
Subjects: LCSH: Academic freedom—United States. | Boycotts—United States—21st century. | Academic freedom—Palestine. | Boycotts—Palestine—21st century. | Arab-Israeli conflict—Social aspects.
Classification: LCC LC72.2 (ebook) | LCC LC72.2 .M35 2018 (print) | DDC 371.1/04—dc23
LC record available at https://lccn.loc.gov/2017030344

Manufactured in the United States of America

26 25 24 23 22 21 20 19 18
10 9 8 7 6 5 4 3 2 1

CONTENTS

OVERVIEW

INTRODUCTION

The Palestinian call for the academic and cultural
boycott of Israel represents a revival of grassroots
and international solidarity movements after the
Oslo Accords. The three principles of Boycott, Divestment,
and Sanctions express a decolonial, antiracist critique
of Israel.

BDS · Academic Boycott · Palestine · Solidarity · Antiracism

CHAPTER I. BOYCOTT AS TACTIC:
HERE AND THERE

The academic boycott draws on the history of the
Montgomery bus boycott, the United Farm Workers
boycott, and the movement that opposed South African
apartheid. The history of the boycott in Palestine
demonstrates that it is central to Palestinian
freedom struggles.

*Montgomery Bus Boycott · Grape Boycott · Antiapartheid
Movement · South Africa · Palestinian Resistance*

CHAPTER 2. THE ACADEMIC BOYCOTT MOVEMENT

The history of the U.S. academic boycott movement is outlined from the formation of the US Campaign for the Academic and Cultural Boycott of Israel to the resolution endorsed by the American Studies Association. Interviews with boycott organizers document the intellectual and political shifts generated by boycott campaigns.

*USACBI · American Studies Association · Academic
Labor · Student Activism*

CHAPTER 3. BACKLASH: THE BOYCOTT AND THE CULTURE/RACE WARS

The backlash against the boycott is an archive of repression that reveals the racial, class, gender, sexual, and national-colonial politics of the culture wars around BDS. The censorship of boycott advocacy exposes the Palestinian exception to academic freedom.

*Backlash · Culture Wars · Anti-Semitism ·
Anti-Zionism · Academic Freedom*

CHAPTER 4. ACADEMIC ABOLITIONISM: BOYCOTT AS DECOLONIZATION

The boycott movement is part of struggles to democratize the neoliberal university, evident in the campaign in defense of Steven Salaita. Interviews with Palestinian scholars and students illustrate that the boycott movement is integral to Palestinian self-determination and Third World internationalism.

*Neoliberal University · Decolonization ·
Internationalism · Steven Salaita*

Introduction

Something unthinkable happened in the United States in the last few years: hundreds of academics—senior scholars and graduate students and untenured faculty—came forth in support of an academic boycott of Israel. Beginning in 2013, the movement to boycott Israeli academic institutions expanded rapidly with one major academic association after another endorsing the boycott and adopting resolutions in solidarity with the Palestinian call for an academic boycott. But this movement emerged several years after Palestinian academics, intellectuals, and activists called for an academic and cultural boycott of Israel, in 2004— and after years of military occupation, failed peace negotiations, ever-expanding and illegal Jewish settlements on Palestinian land, ongoing home demolitions, the building of the Israeli Wall, repression, and military assaults. All of these events and the military occupation of Palestine itself have been endorsed, defended, and funded by Israel's major global ally, the United States. The academic boycott and the Boycott, Divestment, and Sanctions movement are thus embedded in a significant aspect of the U.S. political and historical relationship to the Middle East, and in a particular cultural imaginary of Palestine, Palestinians, and Arabs in general, that has become an increasingly central concern of American studies.

What is the significance of Boycott, Divestment, and Sanctions (BDS) and academic boycott activism, in particular, for the U.S. academy and for social justice movements? What political paradigm is introduced by the academic boycott, and how has this transformed the debate about Palestine-Israel in the United States, and in the academy in particular? I focus on the academic boycott as a social movement that is at the intersection of anti-war, human rights, and global justice organizing in the university and beyond, and increasingly embedded in antiracist, feminist, and queer movements as well. This is a new perspective in the existing literature on the academic boycott, but I will show how it emerges from the politics of BDS when analyzed as a progressive social movement, and from its rich and dramatic history in challenging the status quo in the United States.

WHAT IS THE ACADEMIC BOYCOTT?

The Palestinian Campaign for the Academic and Cultural Boycott of Israel (PACBI)[1] issued a call in 2004 for a boycott by academics and artists until Israel complied with international law by:

1. Ending its occupation and colonization of all Arab lands occupied in June 1967 and dismantling the Wall;
2. Recognizing the fundamental rights of the Palestinian citizens of Israel to full equality; and
3. Respecting, protecting and promoting the rights of Palestinian refugees to return to their homes and properties, as stipulated in UN Resolution 194.

A year later, in 2005, Palestinian civil society organizations—including over 170 political parties, refugee networks, popular resistance committees, trade unions, women's groups, and other segments of the Palestinian national movement—called on the international community to put nonviolent pressure on Israel until it ended its violations of human rights, by enacting Boycott, Divestment, and Sanctions, based on the same three political principles, above. The fact that the academic and cultural boycott of Israel had actually been launched a year earlier than the BDS call is significant because it highlights the centrality of the *academic and cultural* front of the Palestinian struggle against Israeli occupation, colonialism, and apartheid.

This Palestinian-led movement uses the framework of "freedom, justice, and equality," invoking international law and the simple axiom that "Palestinians are entitled to the same rights as the rest of humanity."[2] The BDS movement is thus an antiracist movement calling for racial equality. Significantly, it has also emphasized that the oppression of Palestinians is due to an Israeli "regime of settler colonialism, apartheid, and occupation." These key terms have helped shift the discussion about Palestine-Israel in the United States and provided a new framework. I will elaborate on the terms *apartheid* and *settler colonialism* later, noting for now that the BDS campaign explicitly challenges Israel's displacement and colonization of Palestinians since 1948, its occupation and fragmentation of Palestinian territories, its denial to Palestinian refugees of the right to return to their homes, and its system of racial discrimination subjugating Palestinian citizens of Israel. This denial of racial justice, freedom of movement, and sovereignty has persisted given the relative weakness of the Palestinian national movement in resisting the Israeli state and military, and also because of the failure of the international community to end this oppression. As the BDS movement's statement observes: "Governments fail to hold Israel to account, while corporations and institutions across the world help Israel to oppress Palestinians. Because those in power refuse to act to stop this injustice, Palestinian civil society has called for a global citizens' response of solidarity with the Palestinian struggle for freedom, justice and equality."[3]

This observation for the rationale for BDS points out importantly that while Israel's hegemony is maintained by international collusion, it can also be challenged by international solidarity. Furthermore, it alludes to the powerful point that BDS is actually a strategy of last resort—an admission of failure, in a sense, that nothing else has worked to end Israel's ongoing occupation, injustice, and warfare against the Palestinian people. Israel's impunity is upheld by the support of other states (especially the United States) and international institutions that have either actively defended and funded Israel's occupation and racist regime or refused to sanction it, in contrast to other undemocratic regimes whose human rights violations are routinely denounced by the international community (for example, China, Russia, Egypt, Syria, and Myanmar). It is true that numerous U.N. resolutions have been passed, criticizing the Israeli state's actions and human rights abuses—for what those resolutions are worth, given the United Nations' own limited powers—but the United States has consistently vetoed these. The U.S. government is the most powerful ally of Israel and has provided it with unconditional military, political, and economic support, regardless of which administration is in power. Concomitantly, the issue of Palestinian liberation has historically been suppressed and subjected to censorship in the U.S. academy and public sphere, so there is a legitimization of consistent support for Israel, regardless of its human rights abuses, in the intellectual and cultural realm. This is why the academic and cultural boycott is key.

The BDS movement has ruptured the sanctioned narrative about Palestine-Israel, which occludes the history of colonization and displacement of the Palestinian people. This dominant discourse has for years been established as the norm, which has made it "controversial," including in U.S. universities, to speak about Palestinian national liberation or even, in some instances, to criticize the Israeli occupation. While the lockdown on criticism of Israel has been increasingly challenged in recent years, in the U.S. academy as well as the media, and while more critical research about Palestine-Israel has emerged, scholarship on the social movements that have accompanied these intellectual and discursive shifts is meager. There has been much public debate and media controversy about BDS and the academic boycott, as well as journalistic and activist writing and some edited volumes about the BDS movement,[4] but currently hardly any scholarly work offers an analysis of the historical and political import of the academic boycott. This book is not an exhaustive account of the academic boycott movement in the United States, however, but rather an introduction to the core paradigms, key moments, and significant debates about the movement. It is written from the perspective of someone who has been involved for several years in academic boycott organizing, and in the Palestine solidarity movement at large, and also from the vantage point of a critical ethnic studies scholar who writes about social justice and transnational solidarity activism.

I do not dwell on the cultural boycott of Israel, because those campaigns take place in a different sphere and entail different strategies, generally based on the refusal of international artists to perform in Israel until it complies with the three principles of BDS outlined above, and the rejection of Israeli state sponsorship of cultural production and events. The cultural boycott is crucial for drawing attention both to Israeli apartheid and colonial policies and to its deployment of "soft power" to whitewash these through an international public relations campaign—as was the case in apartheid South Africa—in order to deflect from its violations of human rights.[5] Inspired by the global cultural impact of artists and athletes who refused to participate in events in apartheid South Africa, the cultural and also sports boycott has been growing. Major cultural icons such as Chuck D of Public Enemy and Pulitzer Prize-winning author Junot Diaz have publicly supported the boycott, and NFL players have begun refusing to play in Israel. Numerous consumer and corporate boycott and divestment campaigns have spread like wildfire across the United States and galvanized ordinary citizens and consumers to stop supporting corporations that do business in Israel; for example, Soda Stream, Ahava, Veiolia, G4S, and Airbnb. Another important arena of mobilization is divestment from Israel by churches, which has included a string of successes in the American Friends Service, Mennonite Central Committee, United Church of Christ, Presbyterian Church, and United Methodist Church.

All of these campaigns are extremely significant and integral to the larger BDS movement, but there is much to be said about the academic boycott movement alone, given its meteoric rise in the United States in recent years, and as a campaign that shines a light on important shifts in American studies and in the U.S. university at large. Moreover, this book is not a primer on the Palestine-Israel issue—a vast topic of its own—as much work has already been published on this by specialists. I will not be documenting here the history of Palestinian displacement and dispossession nor the various wars, atrocities, and human rights violations inflicted on Palestinians, which have been extensively recorded elsewhere.

This book theorizes the academic boycott in the context of current debates about rights-based politics, international solidarity, and academic abolitionism and addresses the implications of the boycott for antiracist, anticolonial, feminist, queer, and academic labor movements. To date, the BDS movement has not been adequately researched and analyzed as a *social justice movement*, which is an important theme in American studies. This book fills a gap in existing scholarship, drawing on interviews with scholar-activists deeply engaged with academic boycott organizing, as well as with Palestinian scholars and activists, about the core frames and key strategies of the boycott movement and its implications for the U.S. academy and, of course, justice in Palestine. The BDS movement at large has been the site of significant interracial and cross-movement coalition building, productively linking issues of colonialism, militarization, policing, anti-Blackness, indigeneity, borders, and labor. By all accounts, the boycott has fundamentally transformed the discourse related to Palestine-Israel in the U.S. academy and it has also generated important struggles over issues of censorship, campus governance, and neoliberal university structures.

THE US CAMPAIGN FOR THE ACADEMIC AND CULTURAL BOYCOTT OF ISRAEL

Five years after PACBI was launched in Palestine, a small group of U.S.-based academics founded a national campaign to mobilize support for the boycott call in the United States in 2009, forming USACBI (the US Campaign for the Academic and Cultural Boycott of Israel), in the midst of the 2008–9 Israeli war on Gaza (known as Operation Cast Lead). During that massacre in the besieged territory, in which approximately 1,400 Palestinians were killed (and 13 Israelis), Israel destroyed schools and universities and wreaked havoc on Palestinian society, including its educational institutions and academic life. This attack was part of an ongoing assault on the Palestinian right to education over the years, through closures of Palestinian schools and universities, restrictions on freedom of movement, military violence and incarceration, and repression and humiliation, that has led to a state of "scholasticide," or destruction of the educational environment, in Palestine.[6] USACBI's founders were also responding to the "Open Letter to International Academic Institutions from the Right to Education Campaign" at Birzeit University in Palestine (January 17, 2009), asking the international academic community, unions, and students "to show support and solidarity with the people of Gaza by calling upon their respective governments to impose immediate boycott, divestment and sanctions against the state of Israel."[7] The academic and cultural boycott is a tool that people of conscience the world over can use to refuse complicity with this scholasticide, and sociocide, in Palestine— especially scholars living in the United States, the state that has provided a lifeline to Israel and sustained its regimes of occupation, apartheid, and colonization. When it was launched, USACBI proposed concrete actions that supporters of the boycott could take to withdraw their complicity with Israel and simultaneously support Palestinian academics and students in proactive ways:[8]

> Since Israeli academic institutions (mostly state-controlled) and the vast majority of Israeli intellectuals and academics have either contributed directly to maintaining, defending or otherwise justifying

the above forms of oppression, or have been complicit in them through their silence, we call upon our colleagues to comprehensively and consistently boycott all Israeli academic and cultural institutions as a contribution to the struggle to end Israel's occupation, colonization and system of apartheid, by engaging in the following actions. We aim at the full implementation of all these steps. However, recognizing that different actions may be feasible and appropriate under the many different academic and political circumstances that pertain in US institutions, we urge our colleagues to undertake as many of the following initiatives as possible:

1. Support Palestinian academic and cultural institutions directly without requiring them to partner with Israeli counterparts as an explicit or implicit condition for such support;

2. Encourage your university and college administrations to institute funding for scholarships and fellowships for Palestinian students;

3. Request your administration/president to issue a public statement censuring Israeli destruction of and interference with Palestinian schools and universities, archives and research centers, both in Gaza and throughout occupied Palestine;

4. Work toward the condemnation of Israeli policies by pressing for resolutions to be adopted by academic, professional and cultural associations and organizations;

5. Organize teach-ins or similar events with campus and community organizations at which the campaign for the economic, cultural and academic boycott of Israel can be fully and openly discussed;

6. Refrain from participation in any form of academic and cultural cooperation, collaboration or joint projects with Israeli institutions;

7. Advocate a comprehensive boycott of Israeli institutions at the national and international levels, including suspension of all forms of funding and subsidies to these institutions;

8. Promote divestment and disinvestment from Israel by academic institutions, and place pressure on your own institution to suspend all ties with Israeli universities, including collaborative projects, study abroad, funding and exchanges.

I cite these suggested actions in detail because they show that the boycott is framed by BDS activists as just one element in a larger repertoire of tactics that include positive, proactive programs to support Palestinian scholars and students. This framework also highlights how the boycott can be used to actively promote the Palestinian right to education and academic freedom, including in the United States, a point that has often been obfuscated by the boycott's opponents who have consistently alleged that the boycott undermines academic freedom, as I will discuss in Chapter 3 (see Glossary, s.v. *academic freedom*). Furthermore, it is important to underscore that the academic and cultural boycott complements other BDS strategies, particularly divestment campaigns, which have also spread rapidly across U.S. campuses and churches. I will not be addressing these here, as they deserve a book of their own.

THE POLITICAL PARADIGM OF BOYCOTT

This book focuses on the academic boycott as a transnational social movement that has used the language of global and social justice as well as human rights to reframe the question of Palestinian freedom, and that has historically been suppressed and subjected to censorship in the U.S. academy as well as in the larger U.S. public. The boycott movement has been key to challenging the lockdown on open discussion of Palestine, Israel, and Zionism in the U.S. academy and to transforming the Palestine issue from a marginal cause into a central node of progressive-left academic organizing and campus activism. Palestine was a leftist cause in the 1960s and 1970s during the era of the Third World movement and its anticolonial politics; as I will show in Chapter 1, it was also a contested cause. However, with the consolidation of the special relationship between the United States and Israel and the growing power of the Israel lobby, it was increasingly shunted aside as an issue no one dared to touch for fear of risking the ire of Zionist backlash. The success of the BDS movement, then, has been accompanied by a shift in politics as well as academic thought; over the years, the silencing of criticism of Israel that occurred even in the U.S. left and the erasure or marginalization of Palestinian rights activism led to the unfortunate label, "Progressive Except on Palestine" (or PEP). The Palestine national question could only be framed through a state-sanctioned and euphemistic discourse about "the conflict," and any critique had to be limited to the Israeli military occupation and the Palestinian territories conquered in 1967. The rise of BDS and the boycott movement has been accompanied by and has propelled a new framework that, first, centers Palestinian rights as *integral* to left movements for global and social justice, and second, uses the discourses of settler colonialism, apartheid, and antiracism to challenge foundational narratives of the Israeli state and the displacement of Palestinians beginning in 1948 (see Glossary, s.vv. *settler colonialism; apartheid*).

The call for boycott, and the BDS movement, must be situated in the specific political conjuncture created by the Oslo Accords, signed by Israeli and Palestinian leaders in 1993–94, and the national crisis it created for Palestinians. Oslo represents for many Palestinians the betrayal of the national struggle for self-determination, as it bestowed only limited sovereignty to Palestine, promoted a framework of neoliberal governance, and relegated the newly created Palestinian National Authority to the role of collaborator with Israel in maintaining internal security (that is, in suppressing and disciplining Palestinians).[9] It also compromised on the right of return of refugees and the rights of Palestinian citizens in Israel, creating a framework that gave up on these two groups of Palestinians and splintered the national movement. The Oslo framework rested on the two-state solution and confined a Palestinian state to only 22 percent of historic Palestine; thus, many saw it as leading to the dismembering of Palestine. In addition, Israel's occupying regime maintained control of all borders and generated ambiguous legal categories and forms of identity documentation for the Palestinian population and territories—differentiating between peoples and geographic spaces, for example, in Israel, East/West Jerusalem, Gaza, and West Bank Areas A, B, C. In fact, many commentators observe that the Oslo agreements gave "birth [to] what Jeff Halper has called Israel's 'matrix of control'" in Palestinian areas with the construction and expansion of the Apartheid Wall, (illegal) settlements, (Jewish-only) bypass roads, and checkpoints, strangulating Palestinian life, including educational life.[10]

The emergence of the BDS movement represented a rejection of the Oslo paradigm that was a major factor in the waning and pacification of Palestinian national resistance. Oslo played a role in the decline of mass mobilization in Palestine as it funneled many political activists, including leftists, into a defanged civil society infrastructure based on neoliberal concepts of participatory democracy and "good governance," undermining grassroots movements that were already brutally suppressed by Israel. Oslo led to the Palestinian national community's fragmentation and division into political and administrative units through greater confinement as a result of the expanding Wall and settlements, increased (racial) segregation, and restrictions on freedom of movement by Israel.[11] Palestinians were increasingly disconnected and divided from one another in the bantustans[12] created in the West Bank; in an encircled and peripheralized Jerusalem whose Palestinian residents were subjected to ongoing home demolitions and vicious settler attacks; and in a besieged and blockaded Gaza targeted for serial warfare and recurrent massacres.

The BDS paradigm challenges Oslo as it unifies Palestinians from the West Bank, Gaza, Jerusalem, and inside Israel within a movement based on shared national struggle, as outlined in the three principles of PACBI's call, cited above, challenging Zionist policies of colonization, displacement, and enclosure that have fostered partitioning and political division among Palestinians. It attempts to revive grassroots mobilization, outside of the Palestinian national parties and beyond the language of statehood and neoliberal democracy promoted by the Palestinian Authority. The BDS movement thus represents an important political intervention in the post-Oslo moment of political disillusionment and fatigue and the spatial shrinking of the Palestinian nation. BDS is one plank in an autonomous, grassroots movement to expand the horizon of the Palestinian national movement, and it is one to which many Palestinians of diverse ideological persuasions, religious backgrounds, and generational and geographic locations belong.[13] It is important to situate the emergence of BDS in this historical context of Palestinian national politics, for it is a strategy to revitalize Palestinian collective resistance while creating and reviving circuits of global solidarity, linking the inside and outside of the besieged nation.

The BDS movement has helped resuscitate the politics of international solidarity with Palestine by invoking the discourse of international human rights and international law. This is an important, if complex, move given that the Palestinian national struggle has long been exceptionalized in the United States as undeserving even of liberal human rights and outside of the acceptable parameters of global legal activism.[14] The boycott is also embedded in a politics of left internationalism that flourished in the 1960s and 1970s—the era of Third Worldism and decolonial struggles that linked nations in the global South and left struggles with Palestine—but that has eroded with the decline of these movements, since the 1980s, under a consolidation of neoliberalism and neoconservatism and the dominance of U.S. imperial militarism (see Glossary s.v. *neoliberalism*). In the post–9/11 era and with intensified U.S. military interventions in the Middle East (or West Asia), progressive activists and intellectuals in the United States have increasingly situated Palestine within a framework of antiwar, anti-imperial, feminist, queer, and indigenous politics, viewing the Palestinian struggle as an important front of resistance to U.S. hegemony, in the West Asian region and globally, despite the immense pressure of the Israel lobby and the demonization of Palestine solidarity activists. In this context, the book considers the role the BDS movement has played in providing a language for international solidarity with Palestine that is embedded in an anticolonial and antiracist politics, as well as in rights-based activism.

BDS AND RIGHTS-BASED ACTIVISM

The political principles of the BDS movement are based on human rights, and the strategic power of the call for BDS is its appeal to international human rights and international law. This has been one of the strengths of the boycott movement that has led to its growing power, as well as a thorny issue for leftists and progressives critical of rights-based activism. However, I argue that the boycott movement both rests on and exceeds the language of rights by relying on international human rights law to legitimize the Palestinian struggle, on the one hand, and on the other, by exposing the rightlessness of Palestinians and providing a political paradigm that is radical at its core.[15]

To press on this dualism of rights-based BDS politics, which may on the surface appear paradoxical but which I view as ultimately productive, I would point out that rights are not an abstract concept; rather, they are claimed by specific groups in particular contexts that perform rights claims, in order to make visible forms of violence or acts of erasure. It is certainly true that international human rights institutions are embedded in the racialized world order and distribute and endorse rights unevenly, as critics have rightly pointed out. Clearly, they have failed Palestine, and the Palestinian struggle has generally not been recognized as a legitimate human rights issue within liberal or mainstream U.S. discourse. This has led to a great deal of skepticism about the viability of human rights as a framework for Palestinian national liberation, understandably, especially in Palestine. But as anthropologist Lori Allen argues, drawing on her research with human rights workers in Palestine, this cynicism about human rights can be productive and animates a (Palestinian) political subjecthood that grapples with contradictions and tensions in human rights politics, and that is not duped by the promise of rights but able to operate in multiple political registers.[16] We should thus view the rights discourse deployed by the BDS movement in a more nuanced and strategic way, as playing an important role in highlighting the rights of the rightless, and the power of those who can bestow rights. As the political philosopher Jacques Rancière observes, it is mobilizing this gap, or space of contradiction, that is vital for politics. This is what the BDS movement, and boycott activism, does in mobilizing the contradictions of "Palestinian human rights."[17]

Furthermore, the three principles guiding the BDS movement, cited earlier, address the fundamental contradictions created by a settler colonial state that professes to uphold human rights and democracy while creating an exception of rightlessness for Palestinians. The political framework of USACBI, on which the BDS movement is based, does not offer an explicit solution to the conditions in Palestine-Israel, nor does it propose a one-state versus two-state model; rather, it simply demands equality and justice for Palestinians. The Palestinian call is for an academic and cultural boycott of Israel until it ends its violations of the human rights of the three segments of the fragmented Palestinian nation, namely, refugees denied the right to return; those living under illegal military occupation in the West Bank, Gaza, and East Jerusalem; and Palestinians within the 1948 borders of Israel, subjected to systemic racial discrimination. The focus on these core ethical principles has been unifying for the Palestine solidarity movement outside Palestine, which has been rife with internal divisions, as are most political movements across time and space.

Furthermore, the logical outcome of the three specific demands of the BDS call is that Israel would have to cease its colonial and racially discriminatory policies, end its military occupation, and recognize the right of return of Palestinian refugees. In effect, Israel would no longer be entitled to uphold the supremacy of Jewish citizens over non-Jews and no longer be a colonialist, apartheid, militarized garrison state. The core character of the Zionist state would be transformed (in theory) and the racist logics of Zionism dismantled in order to realize a society based on racial equality, rather than racial and religious hierarchies that regulate life and death. So while the boycott formally relies on a rights-based approach, and it is true that human rights is embedded in a liberal universalist framework of international law, the BDS principles actually use the language of rights to promote an *anti-Zionist and decolonial paradigm* for liberation. These terms are not used in the official BDS call, obviously for strategic reasons, but in its de facto application the boycott paradigm enshrines a radical vision of emancipation.[18] This point has been sometimes misunderstood or distorted—including by some left supporters of Palestine, for whom the boycott is not radical enough, not anticolonial enough, or even not grassroots enough—even though it has been acknowledged by Zionists, who have been increasingly panicked by the powerful threat that BDS poses to Israel. The vicious Zionist backlash, and the shrill claim that BDS aims to destroy Israel, is thus based on an understanding that BDS is a growing grassroots movement that essentially targets the fundamentally racist and colonialist nature of the Israeli state as we know it.[19] As Steven Salaita points out, the BDS framework pivots on "basic rights of self-determination for the Palestinians (e.g. to return, to reside, to participate, and to belong)," and while nowhere does it include "the destruction of Israel," these basic rights are incompatible with the "cultural and biological strictures of Zionism."[20]

In the following chapters, I will discuss how academic boycott organizers and advocates who endorse and promote the BDS principles sometimes do so while exceeding a liberal rights discourse, utilizing the language of apartheid and settler colonialism and framing solidarity via anticolonial, antiracist, anticapitalist, queer, feminist, and indigenous politics. While not all these terms are explicitly invoked in the BDS call, many BDS campaigns have adopted the framework of settler colonialism and apartheid, concepts that travel across national borders and resonate with many who are drawn to anticolonial and antiracist struggles, especially in the United States. Later in the book, I will address how this intersectional politics—invoking race, gender, sexuality, nationalism, class, and indigeneity—has infused the boycott movement and driven successful campaigns based on cross-racial and cross-movement alliances. This broader solidarity and turn to BDS among progressives is precisely what has been so threatening to defenders of Israel, on the right as well as on the left, as I will explore in Chapter 3.

In the first chapter, I situate the academic boycott and BDS in a broader historical context, touching on earlier boycott movements during the civil rights and antiwar struggles in the United States, such as the Montgomery bus boycott and the United Farm Workers grape boycott, as well as the boycott and divestment movement challenging apartheid in South Africa. I also discuss the much less known history of the boycott in Palestine itself, and examples of civil disobedience that have historically been a central part of Palestinian resistance but have been overshadowed in U.S. mainstream discourse by the sensationalized focus on militant Palestinian resistance. This brief historical discussion reframes the narrative about the academic boycott as emerging from the experience of Palestinian anticolonial resistance, and not outside it. Chapter 2 charts a succinct history of the academic boycott movement in the United States, from the founding of USACBI to the first boycott resolution endorsed by the Association of Asian American Studies in 2013 and academic boycott organizing in other national academic associations, particularly the American Studies Association and American Anthropological Association. This chapter combines personal reflections on my own organizing and interviews with some key organizers and supporters of the boycott from various fields, offering for the first time a grounded history of this social movement.

In Chapter 3, I focus on the backlash against BDS, especially attacks on the academic boycott movement, which is part of a well-orchestrated right-wing campaign that has reached the level of state legislation against BDS. Going beyond existing reports that simply document antiboycott campaigns, I use this archive of repression to offer an analysis of the cultural politics and racial/ cultural wars in which the backlash is embedded. Furthermore, I discuss how Palestine is often the funnel of academic repression, in which powerful conservative and Zionist groups collude with university administrations to undermine democratic campus governance and academic employment rights. Building on this discussion, Chapter 4 explores how the boycott movement is on the frontlines of the struggle to democratize the neoliberal university, sparking solidarity among contingent academic workers, dissident and fugitive scholars, and activists. National campaigns, such as the mobilization in support of Palestinian American scholar Steven Salaita, and local labor union campaigns, have highlighted the centrality of the boycott to struggles over academic labor. The boycott, I conclude, is part of the struggle for academic abolitionism, or the movement to decolonize the university, and in support of decolonial struggles in Palestine. This book shows how the academic boycott is not just an act of withdrawal of complicity with settler colonialism and apartheid, or one of academic refusal, but also an act of demanding self-determination and decolonization, here and there.

ONE

Boycott as Tactic

Here and There

The academic boycott continues a tradition that has occurred in a wide range of geographic locations and political contexts, something that is sometimes forgotten in the frenzy over the academic and cultural boycott of Israel and the depiction of the movement as somehow exceptional. In recent years in the United States, for example, there was a boycott of Arizona due to its passing of State Bill 1070 in 2010, which authorized state officials to enforce federal immigration laws and arrest undocumented immigrants on the basis of racial profiling; in addition to grassroots protests, boycott resolutions were passed in other states by the councils of cities such as Los Angeles, Denver, and Minneapolis. In 2016, there was a boycott of North Carolina due to House Bill 2, which nullified a Charlotte city ordinance for gender-neutral public bathrooms (and also local antidiscrimination and wage laws), a campaign that won support from national sports associations, corporations, and major artists. The economic costs and political damage in both cases exerted real pressure on the state legislatures, due largely to the loss of corporate as well as tourist dollars, which led to some rollback of the racist laws. In January 2017, after the election of Donald Trump, there was a call for a boycott and general strike on the day of the presidential inauguration by immigrant rights and antiracist activists, and subsequent calls for strikes and boycotts in solidarity with immigrants, workers, and women. These campaigns of economic and cultural boycott generally focused on domestic issues and pivoted on struggles over race, gender, sexuality, labor, and immigration.

Boycott campaigns in the United States often invoke the inspiring history of the Montgomery bus boycott sparked by Rosa Parks during the civil rights movement, the United Farm Workers (UFW) boycott, and the global boycott of apartheid South Africa. The BDS movement today has in fact explicitly situated itself in this genealogy of boycott, divestment, and sanctions campaigns by oppressed groups and solidarity activists, invoking the South African antiapartheid movement as the primary model for the Palestinian campaign. Of course, the foundational history of the United States includes milestones such as the Boston Tea Party, basically the boycott of British tea by colonists in 1773, so the boycott is not always in the service of anticolonial or indigenous movements, or even progressive politics. In this chapter, I contextualize the academic boycott of Israel in the longer history of boycott as a tactic in social justice organizing that has been used in antiracist, civil rights, and worker struggles, and I gesture to the Montgomery bus boycott and UFW grape boycott, as well as to the role of the boycott in antiapartheid activism in the United States as an example of global solidarity. Given how much has already been written on these boycott movements by specialists in these areas, my focus here will not be a historical review or analysis of these campaigns per se but rather a reflection on what these cases illuminate about boycott as a political tactic: when it is effective, why it is deployed, and how the academic boycott draws on as well as departs from instances of consumer or transit boycott. I will also address the often ignored history of boycotts in Palestine over the years, highlighting the ways this strategy has long been used by Palestinians in their resistance to colonization and occupation. The academic (as well as consumer) boycott of Israel has been recreated in the twenty-first-century BDS movement and shaped by the experiences and lessons of boycott campaigns elsewhere. I will discuss how debates over the boycott speak to questions of reform and radicalism, violence and nonviolence, solidarity and self-determination.

THE BUS BOYCOTT

One of the most iconic instances of boycott actions as part of a social movement in the United States is the by-now legendary bus boycott in Montgomery, Alabama—a milestone of the civil rights struggle. In December 1955, Rosa Parks, an African American woman and NAACP organizer, was arrested for sitting in the Whites-only section of a municipal bus and refusing to move to the back, sparking a boycott of local buses as part of an expanding protest against racial segregation on city buses. In 1956, approximately 90 percent of Montgomery's Blacks refused to use the buses, as part of a collective campaign led by civil rights leaders such as Dr. Martin Luther King Jr., the Rev. Ralph Abernathy, and Bayard Rustin.[1] For over a year, Blacks in Alabama refused to ride in the back of segregated buses, instead walking, carpooling, or taking taxis.[2] This movement against "apartheid-style social relations" in the Jim Crow era spread to other cities in the deep South and became internationally famous, King becoming a symbol of antiracism for "millions of colored people across the world."[3] In 1956, the Supreme Court outlawed racial segregation on Montgomery buses, even as the boycott movement and direct actions were met with violent backlash by militant Whites and racist mobs, aided by state guards.

As Manning Marable documents, the bus boycott was not the first such action waged by African Americans protesting racism.[4] As early as 1865, abolitionist Sojourner Truth led Blacks in Washington, DC, in a boycott of segregated public transportation facilities. In the 1940s, Adam Clayton Powell led a series of popular boycotts for Black jobs and greater social and welfare services.[5] Boycotts to desegregate lunch counters and schools in midwestern and northern cities were organized by groups such as the Congress of Racial Equality, which focused on nonviolent direct action. The campaign to test desegregation laws on buses in the upper South in 1947, as part of the Journeys of Reconciliation, were forerunners of the historic Freedom Rides movements of the 1960s, as Marable notes.[6] A few days after Parks's arrest in Montgomery, King gave a speech at the Holt Street Baptist Church in which he lauded Parks and proclaimed why the boycott and other nonviolent direct actions were necessary:

> You know my friends there comes a time when people get tired of being trampled over by the iron feet of oppression. There comes a time my friends when people get tired of being flung across the abyss of humiliation.... There comes a time when people get tired of being pushed out of the glittering sunlight of life's July and left standing amidst the piercing chill of an Alpine November. We are here, we are here this evening because we are tired now.... The only weapon we have in our hands this evening is the weapon of protest.[7]

King powerfully observes that resistance, including civil disobedience, emerges from the sheer necessity of needing to fight oppression, and the boycott, like other strategies, is the produce of years of fatigue, which leave people with no choice but to use this weapon. As King also eloquently suggests, boycotts are tools that ordinary people can use in their daily lives to protest a powerful status quo, by physically using their body as an instrument of antiracist protest, as Parks and others did in Montgomery or as students sitting at lunch counters did in Greensboro, North Carolina. King wrote in his famed "Letter from a Birmingham City Jail" after intentionally letting himself be arrested at a demonstration in April 1963: "we had no alternative except that of preparing for direct action, whereby we would present our very bodies as a means of laying our case before the local and national community."[8] The boycott need not always be physically embodied, for it can also be enacted through a rejection of participation in spaces or institutional structures that are complicit with or represent oppression, or a refusal to purchase consumer goods—as in the case of the boycott of products by companies doing business with apartheid South Africa or, in an earlier era, Gandhi's boycott of British goods in India in the independence struggle.

As a tactic, boycott is a powerful means of popular resistance, or what activists call people's power. As Clayborne Carson observes, the Montgomery bus boycott and sit-ins demonstrated that "people without resources and specialized skills could play decisive roles in achieving social change" and were part of a "mass movement that produced its own leaders and ideas."[9] Significantly, the BDS movement, too, is a grassroots, decentralized movement that has enabled many groups and individuals without economic and political power, who lack resources, to engage in collective protests, regardless of political affiliation and without a hierarchical leadership structure. As Carson notes, the many acts of civil disobedience and protest for civil rights in the

1960s were not necessarily always directed by emblematic leaders such as King or Malcolm X; they were part of a mass movement that was propelled by hundreds of individuals who were inspired to act, and that spread like wildfire across the United States, drawing in White solidarity activists and students.[10]

King and the Southern Christian Leadership Council framed their protests using Christian symbols and the language of Christian brotherhood, love, and nonviolence. While this contrasted with the radical political frameworks of Black Power groups such as the Student Nonviolent Coordinating Committee (SNCC) and the Black Panther Party, the nonviolence of direct action tactics, including the boycott, gave participants in civil rights activism "a sense of moral superiority, an emotional release through militancy."[11] This is applicable to the BDS movement, too, which is explicitly articulated through the language of nonviolent resistance to Israel's violent occupation and racial segregation policies; boycott activists can claim a moral edge over defenders of oppression in affirming principles of social justice and racial equality. Of course, what is different and complicated in this case is that BDS campaigns and Palestine solidarity activists are challenging a regime founded as a state for the Jewish people, and so are often branded as anti-Semitic by antiboycott and Zionist critics, despite the explicitly antiracist principles of the BDS movement. Proponents of BDS come from a variety of religious backgrounds, however, and include atheists and agnostics as well as Jewish advocates. It is also the case that various faith-based Palestine solidarity groups are involved in BDS campaigns, such as Sabeel, Jewish Voice for Peace, and American Muslims for Palestine, and there has been a powerful call for BDS by Palestinian Christians shaped by the tradition of liberation theology known as Kairos.[12]

The academic boycott springs from a history of civil disobedience, as well as of Third World and anticolonial politics. The
BDS movement appeals to people of conscience of diverse racial,
religious, and national backgrounds to engage in international
solidarity, and in this it resonates across time and space with the
internationalism of civil rights activists who situated their freedom struggle in the global context of decolonization movements
in Africa and the Third World. This Third Worldism was particularly evident in the politics of Malcolm X and Black Power
nationalists who demanded a radical transformation of the U.S.
state, which they viewed as a racist, imperial nation-state, and
who did not view legal desegregation and nonviolence as the
means to achieve true racial equality and democracy, unlike
the NAACP and Southern Christian Leadership Conference
headed by King.[13] For Marable, in fact, the boycott and other
nonviolent actions in the civil rights struggle achieved limited
racial equality but did not represent a real challenge to U.S.
imperial racism and capitalism, as articulated by radical activists in SNCC and the Black Panther Party, even though their
members also engaged in acts of civil disobedience. Here I will
not delve into the ideological divide between reform and radicalism, which has already been extensively discussed; I want to
address a different if related point, that nonviolent direct actions
in the civil rights movement posed a threat to the social order
and were targeted for backlash by racist defenders of the status
quo, as in the case of the Israel boycott. Desegregation campaigns in the United States were brutally repressed, including
with the aid of state governments, and civil rights activists and
leaders had to contend with harassment, intimidation, physical
assaults, bombings, and even assassination.

In fact, nonviolent civil disobedience was portrayed as being too radical by White liberals, as King reflected in the famed letter from the Birmingham jail:

> I have almost reached the regrettable conclusion that the Negroes' great stumbling block in the stride toward greater freedom is not the "White Citizens' 'Counciler'" or the Ku Klux Klanner, but the white moderate who is more devoted to order than justice: ... who constantly says, "I agree with you in the goal you seek, but I can't agree with your methods of direct action": who paternalistically feels he can set the timetable for another man's freedom; who lives by the myth of time and who constantly advises the Negro to wait until a "more convenient season."[14]

King's pointed rebuke here of White "moderates" and liberals who profess solidarity with African Americans yet denounce their tactics as untimely, claiming to know better than the oppressed what strategies they should use for their liberation, has a painful echo in the contemporary pronouncements of Jewish liberals, and even leftists, who have condemned BDS, and the academic boycott in particular, as an inappropriate strategy for Palestinians in their struggle for freedom. Well-respected Jewish American leftists, such as Noam Chomsky and Norman Finkelstein, who support Palestinian rights (and have themselves been attacked for doing so) have publicly criticized the boycott and BDS movement as it has gained momentum in the United States.[15] This has been damaging to the BDS movement as it confuses people on the left, especially, given that these prominent progressive intellectuals, who have wide followings, have asserted their authority to discredit the tactic of boycott called for by Palestinians, and it implies that the Palestinian people are incapable of deciding what is an appropriate form of resistance.

Over and over again, advocates of the academic boycott—including myself—have been told by progressives, both Jewish and non-Jewish, that while they support an end to the occupation and oppose Israel's wars and discriminatory policies, they cannot endorse the boycott, because it is not effective, is misguided in its target, and because now is simply not the right time. So when exactly *is* the right time for rejecting complicity with an oppressive state? What does it mean to suggest that an occupied and oppressed people do not have the right to determine the best form of resistance and solidarity in their own struggle for freedom? For Finkelstein and Chomsky, however, it is apparent that one of the main sources of their unwillingness to come out in support of a Palestinian-led call for international civil society to engage in BDS is an anxiety about what this means for the future of Israel; underlying this is a denial that there are South African-style apartheid policies inflicted on Palestinians, cloaked in accusations that Palestinians (according to Finkelstein) are blindly following a BDS "cult."[16]

There are also detractors among Palestinians and Arabs who are critical of BDS, for different reasons, such as that it is not radical enough and is based on a liberal paradigm of human rights. However, the racial politics of location and privilege cannot be overlooked in the debates about BDS, as in King's eloquent criticism of the paternalistic White moderate. I will elaborate more on the critique of the academic boycott of Israel, from the left and the right, in Chapter 3, and reflect on the implications of the challenge the boycott poses to academic liberalism and the dominant notions of academic freedom it upholds. Here I want to tease out the racial fissures that historically inform the boycott movement and politics of Palestine solidarity in the United States, and that can partly be traced back to the civil rights era and the boycott of apartheid South Africa.

THE "SOUTH AFRICA MOMENT": THE SPLIT OVER APARTHEID

The civil rights struggle was accompanied by a fractious debate between moderates and radicals over solidarity and self-determination in relation to the boycott and civil disobedience. Black leftists who posed a radical challenge to U.S. imperial racism and who were antiwar, anti-imperialist, were *also* in some cases anti-Zionist; they opposed Black Cold War liberals, some of whom supported Zionism and Israel.[17] In fact, one of the striking splits that occurred among civil rights activists and within the New Left in the 1960s was between Jewish Americans who supported Zionism, and the leftists, including African Americans, who increasingly challenged Israel after the 1967 Israeli-Arab War, which some antiwar activists likened to the Vietnam War.[18] While civil rights leader Bayard Rustin and labor organizer A. Philip Randolph founded the Black Americans to Support Israel Committee, radical Black activists, such as those in SNCC and the Black Panther Party, identified with the Palestinian freedom struggle as based on self-determination and resistance to racial oppression and colonization, principles that resonated with their own increasingly anticolonial and internationalist framework.[19] In its 1967 newsletter, SNCC published a landmark statement exemplifying this stance, which condemned "Israel as a colonial state" and identified with Palestinians as "victims of racial subjugation."[20] In doing this, they broke with the sympathy for Zionism among some Black leaders, such as those in the NAACP, who had publicly declared support for Israel since 1948; according to Robin Kelley, the latter associated it with a nation-building project opposed to racial oppression, an association based on the power of Zionism's foundational mythologies and the context of the Holocaust.[21] The schism on the left between Black radicals and antiapartheid activists on the one hand, and Jewish Zionists on the other, widened in the context of Israel's strengthened alliance with apartheid South Africa, a political realignment that pitted Israel against Black liberation movements. For example, in 1970 members of the American Committee on Africa published a letter in the *New York Times* countering a previous statement by Black Americans supporting Israel; the letter expressed solidarity with their "Palestinian brothers and sisters" and described both Israel and South Africa as "white settler states."[22]

The growth of the antiapartheid movement in solidarity with Black South Africa in the 1960s, and the call to boycott the apartheid state that spread globally, was a moment when Jewish Zionists became alienated from left movements and human rights campaigns, as some prioritized uncritical allegiance to Israel and labeled Jewish Americans who did not as traitors.[23] The Sharpeville massacre in South Africa in 1960 coincided with the spread of the sit-in movement in the United States and the founding of SNCC; it was a moment when opposition to apartheid infused civil rights and antiracist struggles. Black activist groups picketed South African consulates in the United States, and the Emergency Action Conference on South Africa called for a consumer and financial boycott of South Africa.[24] Students on college campuses erected shantytowns to protest South African apartheid, in some cases making linkages to Palestine-Israel. The backlash this provoked from supporters of Israel (such as at

Johns Hopkins University, where the mock shantytown was actually burned down) pivoted on a shift in the vocabulary that was now applied to Israel, for it was increasingly described as an *apartheid state* and likened to South Africa.[25] This was a significant rupture of the notion that Israel was a nation founded through a struggle for national liberation, one that could be likened to colonized nations.

Critics of Israel challenged the foundational myths of Zionism and Israel's alliances with racist states such as apartheid South Africa, if not also its dispossession and displacement of Palestinians and ongoing racial discrimination against an Arab (that is, non-White) population as a form of apartheid. As Heidi Grunebaum, who is Jewish South African, observes: "One only has to examine the fifty or so laws and legal amendments passed by Israel's Knesset that apportion hierarchically and qualitatively differential civil rights, entitlements and privileges to Jewish Israelis as distinct from the restrictions on Palestinian citizens of Israel. Together with a military administration and fractured 'discontiguity' of Israel's spatial regime governing all aspects of Palestinian life on the occupied West Bank and Israel's blockade of Gaza by land, sea and air, the state envisions and administers Palestinian life very differently to Jewish Israeli life."[26] Given this context, it is not surprising that South Africans struggling against apartheid also stood in solidarity with the Palestinian liberation struggle, and as South African writer and activist Salim Vally reflects, "The Palestine Liberation Organization (PLO) became a symbol of resistance for most South Africans" in this era.[27]

When anticolonial and antiracist activists condemned apartheid in South Africa and later applied this concept to the Zionist state, they were not simply using a rhetorical analogy but challenging a specific structure of institutionalized racial discrimination that came to be defined by international law and recognized as warranting sanctions. In 1973, the International Convention on the Suppression and Punishment of the Crime of Apartheid condemned apartheid as entailing "inhuman acts committed for the purpose of establishing and maintaining domination by one racial group of persons over any other racial group of persons and systematically oppressing them."[28] In their coedited book *Against Apartheid: The Case for Boycotting Israeli Universities,* Ashley Dawson and Bill Mullen point out that "Israeli apartheid is founded on three cornerstones that closely resemble those of apartheid in South Africa"; that is, first, an edifice of racial control built on laws codifying a racial hierarchy of groups with different rights and privileges and upholding White superiority; second, racial segregation of the population in geographic spaces, including the establishment of racial enclaves or "Bantustans" in which Blacks were forced to live; and third, the use of "security" for legalizing incarceration, torture, and censorship.[29] Dawson and Mullen point out, as have others, that the Israeli state has similar sets of laws for consolidation of racial privilege, segregation (or "bantustanization," making the analogy to South Africa), and repression in the name of Israeli security.[30]

Many scholars have also pointed out that the analogy between South African and Israeli apartheid does not suggest that the two systems are identical; for one, "In apartheid South Africa, a White minority sought to maintain domination over a Black majority. In Israel, by contrast, a Jewish majority engages in discriminatory treatment of a minority of Palestinians in Israel itself, as well as discriminatory treatment of Palestinians under a military occupation."[31] Two, as Ben White has argued, a key difference is that "[w]hile in apartheid South Africa, the settlers exploited the labor power of the dispossessed natives, in the case of Israel, 'the native population was to be eliminated; exterminated or expelled rather than exploited.' ... Israel needs the land, but without the people."[32] This relationship to the indigenous (Palestinian) population speaks to the settler colonial logics of Zionism (see Glossary). But as scholars of South Africa, such as T.J. Tallie, underscore, "the analogy between the two countries remains significant as both of their governmental systems, from the point of view of the colonized, are oppressive minority regimes. Both regimes use recourses to broader nationalism or disingenuous claims to universal democracy to only allow full citizenship and access to power for a significant minority of the population." Notably, in 2002, Archbishop Desmond Tutu made an eloquent statement after his visit to Palestine-Israel, describing what he saw as apartheid and lamenting that "it reminded me so much of what happened to us black people in South Africa."[33] This statement by a much-venerated Black South African, antiapartheid activist was a key moment in the establishment of the framework of apartheid in relation to Israel, even if it continued to be contested by defenders of Israel—who also attacked former U.S. president Jimmy Carter when he published *Palestine: Peace Not Apartheid.*[34]

The "South Africa moment" in the United States, when public opposition to South African apartheid gained momentum in the 1960s, was also a turning point in the discourse about Palestine-Israel that fueled solidarity among leftists and people of color with Palestinians, rather than with Israelis. This turn to Palestinian solidarity was strengthened by shocking incidents that highlighted the growing alliance between Israel and South Africa, such as the visit of South African prime minister John Vorster to Israel in 1976 during the Soweto Uprising.[35] In fact, in

1961 South African prime minister Hendrik Verwoerd had "approvingly stated that 'Israel like South Africa is an apartheid state.'"[36] Suturing Israel to Africa through the paradigm of apartheid was thus not just a rhetorical move, given the significant material and political collaboration between the two states. For example, Israel not only helped South Africa evade international sanctions but was an "important arms supplier" to the apartheid regime, even providing nuclear weaponry as well as a trade partner, as Israeli companies were established in many South African bantustans.[37]

The adoption of the language of apartheid in relation to Israel in this period was also strengthened by a growing international discourse challenging Zionism as a form of racism, illustrated most visibly by the resolution passed by the United Nations General Assembly in 1975 and by the statement passed at the UN World Conference on Women in Mexico City, which condemned colonialism and racism as well as Zionism. UN Resolution 3379 declared Zionism a form of racism, provoking deepened splits between Black and Jewish Americans as well as within the women's movement.[38] In the 1970s and 1980s, Zionist feminists were alienated from Third World feminists, such as the radical anti-imperial feminists in the Alliance against Women's Oppression, in San Francisco, who associated Israel with apartheid and who denounced support for Zionism in liberal and radical segments of the women's movement. Yet for anti-Zionist Jewish feminists, such as Eleanor Roffman of Feminist Jews for Justice, in Boston, it "was the language of the antiapartheid movement, specifically, that lent itself to a deeper examination of what was happening in Israel."[39] The framework of apartheid clarified for many Third World activists and leftists that support for the Palestinian liberation struggle was a stance against racial oppression in a global context.

The movement for boycott, divestment, and sanctions challenging apartheid South Africa is thus significant not only for providing a repertoire of tactics and strategies for the later BDS movement in solidarity with Palestine, but also for offering a discursive framework that evolved into an ideological arsenal for articulating opposition to Zionism as antiracism. Yet highlighting the resemblance between apartheid South Africa and Israel also created an intense schism on the left, one that presaged contemporary controversies over criticisms of Israel that describe Zionism as racism or Israel as an apartheid state. In Chapter 3, I discuss why the principles of the boycott are so threatening to Zionists, and how it continues to fuel powerful movements based on Black-Palestinian solidarity and the framework of racial justice and decolonization. The point to stress here is how the internationalism in which the contemporary BDS movement is embedded draws on a genealogy of anticolonial and antiracist solidarities that linked Palestine not just to the United States but also to other global sites of racial struggle, especially South Africa.

THE GRAPE BOYCOTT

The academic boycott as a tactic draws on histories of global antiracist solidarity and struggles based on popular resistance by oppressed groups who used whatever means they had in their power, including the withdrawal of complicity with institutions embedded in systems of domination. Labor movements are a primary arena in which the boycott has been used, most notably in the United States by the United Farm Workers (UFW) in the grape boycott from 1965 to 1978. The boycott has a long tradition in the United States that can be traced back to the Boston Tea Party, a boycott of English tea by settlers in the North American colonies. It is noteworthy that consumer boycotts can be used not only in the progressive spirit of social justice but also in the service of economic nationalism; for example, the various "Buy American" campaigns to boycott foreign goods to shore up the U.S. economy and protect U.S. corporations from foreign competition over the years, including after 9/11. The boycott is thus not intrinsically a tool of the left—it is a tactic, not an ideology, so its politics depends very much on the context of its deployment. This becomes important in discussions of the academic boycott and BDS.

In the case of the UFW boycott of grapes to demand better working conditions for farmworkers, Chicano labor leader Cesar Chavez transformed the boycott into a social movement, similar to abolitionists who called for a boycott of southern-made textiles as a protest against slavery, and of course the Montgomery bus boycott challenging racial segregation. Yet as Matt Garcia notes, "the boycott had long been regarded as a tool of last resort" in the labor movement, secondary to strikes and marches, which were actions over which organizers had more control.[40] For the farmworker movement, the grape boycott campaign also meant a spatial shift, as it entailed organizing in sites far removed from the rural areas where farm labor was based. But the boycott represented a new opportunity for Chavez and the UFW, as Garcia argues, connecting Mexican and Filipino farm laborers to urban consumers and infusing union organizing with the ethos of social justice.[41] It also connected different worker constituencies with longshoremen refusing to unload grapes in San

Francisco, thus challenging the notion that dockworkers did not share the concerns of agricultural workers. In fact, in the context of the BDS movement today, it is notable that the famed International Longshore Workers Union (ILWU) endorsed the "Block the Boat" campaign during the Israeli war on Gaza in the summer of 2014 and refused to unload Israeli ships at the Oakland, Long Beach, and Los Angeles ports;[42] this bold campaign was an echo of the ILWU's refusal to unload South African cargo at the Oakland docks in 1984.[43] The academic boycott has also enacted a similar spatial shift by reorienting the front of the Palestine solidarity movement to the academy, thus drawing scholars and students into the BDS movement by targeting Israeli academic institutions—not just Israeli corporations or multinational companies doing business in Israel, which are the targets of economic boycott and divestment campaigns.

In the grape boycott campaign, the UFW created an "effective boycott network that stretched across North America" with "boycott houses" where volunteers organized locally and gained experience organizing.[44] This network, which not only spanned the United States but also spread to Canada and Europe, internationalized the grape boycott, akin to the ways the academic boycott has seeded campaigns in far-flung campuses across the United States and around the world and is not based in any one physical location. The grape boycott posed a significant challenge to grape growers, who though powerful and wealthy, ultimately lost the battle of public opinion to the UFW, as they found themselves on the "other side of a new generation that now began to question the war, the treatment of racial minorities, and the responsibility of the educated class to society."[45] This is an important point about the efficacy of the academic boycott of Israel as well, for it is an instrument that clarifies political lines. The academic boycott is at its core a tool that ruptures the dominant narrative about Israel as a lone, democratic, civilized state in a sea of barbaric Arab nations threatening its existence, instead highlighting its role as a powerful, well-funded, highly militarized state that has ruthlessly suppressed and encaged the relatively weak Palestinian population and occupied their lands, in violation of international human rights, and that has waged wars against neighboring Arab states.

So as with the grape boycott's challenge to grape growers in an earlier era, the more powerful Zionist lobby has been losing ground in the war of legitimacy waged by BDS—by waging what Antonio Gramsci would call the "war of position."[46] This refers to the struggle to challenge dominant cultural beliefs, in contrast to the "war of maneuver," or open war and armed attack, and is key to understanding the successes of the boycott as a social movement that has challenged the hegemony of Israel, which is based on a set of popular beliefs that normalize its policies (see Glossary, s.v. *war of position/war of maneuver*). The moral fulcrum of the discourse about Palestine-Israel has begun to shift (as it did in an earlier moment of internationalist solidarity) to greater sympathy for the Palestinian people and their freedom struggle, especially in a younger generation of Americans, including Jewish Americans.[47]

The grape boycott also highlights, as did the Montgomery bus boycott, that the effectiveness of the boycott is due to its popular nature. As Chavez said in 1968, "The key to the boycott is people." In a rousing speech to volunteers at a UFW retreat, the labor leader said: "You're building an army of supporters, and you need to find a way to get the people on your side. An organizer will find a way to do the boycott. You can tell me the boycott's difficult. You can tell me they're spitting on you in

L.A.; that they're telling you to go back to Mexico, that they're calling you a Communist. You can tell me it's cold in Toronto. I understand that. But don't tell me it can't be done. 'Si se puede!'"[48] This speech captures the spirit of the academic boycott movement as well: the belief that despite the uphill struggle and the vicious, well-orchestrated backlash by defenders of Israel against BDS advocates, it *has* been possible. The boycott and BDS movement have been sustained by a belief that ordinary people, if educated about the reality in Palestine-Israel, will be won over to supporting Palestinian rights. The "key ... is people," for that is all that the underfunded, besieged Palestinian solidarity movement has on its side.

The key, too, to the success of the BDS movement, as with the grape boycott, is that it fundamentally rests on a moral argument—about freedom, equality, and decolonization. The boycott movement has (re)introduced antiracist and anticolonial paradigms to the Palestine solidarity movement, frameworks that resonate with U.S. publics who are especially attuned to the language of antiracism and racial equality. The grape boycott, too, was not simply focused on labor issues. As Curtis Marez observes, "Chavez and other union organizers envisioned the farm worker movement as part of a larger struggle of poor people against wealth and power and viewed the Southwest as part of the global south. Chavez famously translated Gandhi's strategies of nonviolent resistance in British India and Martin Luther King's strategies in Selma to the Southwestern agricultural fields."[49] Furthermore, as Marez points out, the UFW also worked in alliance with the Black Panther Party, which supported the boycott of Safeway in Oakland, for example, partly because the grocery store refused to support the Panthers' free breakfast program.[50] Despite the focus on Chavez's commitments to nonviolence, as Marez argues, the UFW also expressed a militant, radical Third Worldist politics that was variously inspired by Zapatismo, Maoism, and the movement against the war in Vietnam, a politics that has been deemphasized in popular representations of the UFW.

Yet the UFW's politics was contradictory, as Marez demonstrates, for it posed a revolutionary, popular challenge to agribusiness while also espousing Cold War anticommunism and social conservatism inflected by Catholicism. In addition to Chavez's controversial support for the anticommunist Filipino dictator Ferdinand Marcos, he in fact publicly supported Israel during the 1973 Arab-Israeli War and opposed the 1975 U.N. resolution condemning Zionism as racism, comparing oppressed Mexicans to Israelis. Ironically, Mexico was one of the states that had voted in *support* of the U.N. resolution on Zionism (prompting Jewish American organizations to call for a tourism boycott of Mexico—an interesting historical twist on boycott activism!).[51] Marez also points out that Chavez's support for Zionism undermined the UFW's alliance with the Black Panthers; these conflicting political stances and affiliations are also highlighted by the fact that there were Arab members of the UFW, given that Yemeni farmworkers were very visible in the areas where the UFW organized.

Finally, Garcia rightly notes that current antiracist campaigns, such as the boycott of Arizona due to its racial profiling of Mexicans and immigrants of color (SB1070), still draw on the genealogy of the grape boycott, and that the grape boycott "succeeded due to constant organizing and adapting of strategies that propelled the movement forward," as in the case of the academic boycott.[52] Boycott as a tactic can be framed in multiple ways—as nonviolent or militant, as site-specific or spatially mobile—and its flexibility, clearly, is its strength. This holds as well with the BDS movement.

THE BOYCOTT IN PALESTINE

What is much less discussed than either the grape boycott or the Montgomery bus boycott as informing the genealogy of the academic boycott is the history of the boycott as a tool of popular resistance in Palestine itself. As Omar Barghouti, the cofounder of PACBI and a prominent Palestinian BDS leader, points out, the Palestinian BDS campaign is based on "a comprehensive rights-based approach, rooted in a century of popular and civic struggle against settler colonialism."[53] This virtual erasure of the history of Palestinian civil disobedience and the Palestinian tradition of boycott is due in large part to the general absence of knowledge about Palestinian history in the United States, and to the skewed public discourse in the U.S. mainstream media that is typically biased toward Israel and heavily focused on sensationalized representations of Palestinian violence.

In this persistently Orientalist worldview of Palestine, which has only deepened since the events of September 11, 2001, despite the recurrent Israeli wars on Gaza and military invasions of the West Bank since then, the only means that Palestinians presumably use in resisting Israeli occupation and oppression are savage acts of suicide bombing. The Palestinian is, if anything, the prototypical terrorist in the mainstream U.S. public imagination, a racist caricature thoroughly critiqued by the renowned Palestinian theorist of Orientalism, Edward Said.[54] Orientalism is the system of thought that historically created a binary between the "Orient" (East) and the "Occident" (West), relying on cultural and civilizational distinctions that characterize the Oriental "other" as inherently irrational, violent, hypersensual, and spiritual, and a product of a repressive and barbaric culture, thus justifying Western colonization (see Glossary, s.v. *Orientalism*).

Mainstream media depictions of the Intifadas (or popular uprisings) in Palestine crystallized the trope of the Palestinian as fanatical suicide bomber or, at best, thrower of stones against Israeli tanks, propagating the notion that Palestinians and Muslims are inherently anti-Semitic, anti-American, and antiwestern. (Even Said himself was demonized for throwing the famed stone over the Israeli-Lebanese border into his occupied homeland, before his death.)

Thus, the arsenal of Palestinian resistance is reduced in the public imaginary to a narrow repertoire of stone throwing, if by the diminutive David against a powerful Goliath; the firing of rockets by Hamas from the besieged Gaza Strip, however ineffective against the disproportionately more powerful Israeli military; and suicide bombings, supposedly celebrated by a perverse cult of Muslim violence. Civil disobedience is seen in this Orientalist worldview as inherently un-Palestinian and un-Arab (as well as un-Muslim), as it is conflated generally with Martin Luther King Jr. and Mahatma Gandhi. The boycott is thus associated only with non-Arab and non-Muslim emancipation struggles in the public imagination of nonviolent resistance to oppression.

Given the terribly reductive and deeply Orientalist imagery of Palestinian resistance, it is little wonder that very few in the United States—including even progressives and scholars— know that the boycott is part of a long history of Palestinian civil disobedience that can be traced at least to the 1930s, when Palestinians were engaged in popular protest against both the British Mandate and Zionist regime in Palestine.[55] As Mazin Qumsiyeh notes, the boycott is described in Arabic by Palestinians as *muqawama sha'biya*—which means popular resistance rather than nonviolent resistance—a term he argues is preferred to the latter due to its connotations of a more complex and empowering notion of resistance.[56] Qumsiyeh has written a comprehensive and fascinating history of Palestinian popular resistance to colonization dating to protests in Palestine of Ottoman rule in the nineteenth century and Palestinian calls for noncooperation with Zionists to challenge land expropriation in the 1880s–90s.[57]

For example, Palestinians called for sanctions against Zionist settlers in the Ottoman parliament, as Qumsiyeh notes, and they later boycotted Lord Balfour's visit to Palestine in 1925 as part of protests in support of self-determination and against the Balfour Declaration of 1917 (in which Britain supported establishing a Jewish homeland in Palestine, despite having no jurisdiction over the territory).[58] In 1935, there was a Palestinian call for a boycott of foreign goods and civil disobedience in defiance of British colonial laws. For example, Sami Al-Sarraj wrote in 1935: "Come, oh Arabs, let us displace the laws one time … there is nothing that forces you to buy products of foreigners and certainly not products of your enemies."[59] In 1936, there was also a tax boycott to challenge Zionist land expropriation and settlement, as well as mass protests and general strikes, at a moment when many Palestinians were being economically eviscerated and displaced from their lands due to Jewish migration.[60] In fact, the first use in Palestine of the slogan "No Taxation without Representation" was during the tax revolt spurred by the Arab Car Owners and Drivers Committee in 1936, as part of a wave of grassroots resistance to Zionist colonization and transfer of Palestinians lands to European settlers, and in support of a democratic government.[61]

BDS is thus not just a twentieth-century phenomenon in Palestine, but is deeply embedded in the long history of Palestinian popular resistance. At the same time, one must not read anachronistically into the past but situate the boycott in specific historical moments with their particular circumstances of oppressive rule and popular mobilization. The tax boycott mentioned above, for example, took place in the context of the Great Revolt of 1936–39 in which five thousand Palestinians were killed by the British, hundreds were imprisoned, and many homes were demolished, again by the British.[62] After the creation of the state of Israel in 1948, with the collusion of western powers, various forms of popular boycott emerged among different segments of the Palestinian population as part of ongoing grassroots resistance. As Qumsiyeh and many others have observed, these actions stem from Palestinian insistence on the concept of *sumuud,* or steadfastness, a broad notion that goes beyond the binary of violent/nonviolent resistance and instead enshrines the idea of deep resilience.

There have also been state-sponsored boycotts in support of Palestine, such as that called for by oil-producing Arab regimes who refused to export oil to countries supporting the Israeli occupation in 1973–74. But the grassroots boycott campaigns in Palestine are the most significant, and form the historical context for the global BDS movement, particularly during the first Intifada, or popular uprising, of 1987–91. The Palestinian national leadership of the Intifada issued a call for boycott, civil disobedience, and strikes in 1988.[63] As Qumsiyeh notes, grassroots committees in Palestine—which included women's committees, youth committees, agricultural committees, transportation committees, and prisoners' committees—organized locally and helped create a coordinated mass movement that was the backbone of popular resistance against Israel. This included a boycott of Israeli products in order to exact a price on the occupation, and a withholding of Palestinian labor, a refusal to comply with the Israeli court system, and hunger strikes by Palestinian prisoners in Israeli jails. Importantly, the first Intifada also involved strikes and demonstrations by Palestinians *inside* Israel, despite the systematic repression of that community since 1948. In fact, the Palestinian nationalist party, Abna al-Balad, boycotted Israeli elections despite the violent reprisals against protests by Palestinian citizens of Israel, such as the killing of nonviolent protesters in October 2000 (known as "Black October") and other acts of collective punishment and political repression of Palestinians in Israel.[64]

What is powerful about this history of the Palestinian-led boycott (and divestment) movement is that it was predicated on the principle of self-determination and represents an attempt by Palestinians to establish their own leadership and social order as they rejected the Israeli occupation and colonial regime's authority. The boycott was sustained and supported by an autonomous, mass-based movement that was highly organized—for example, women's committees ensured a nutritious diet while maintaining the boycott; the provisions committees helped food supplies reach enclosed areas; the commercial committee strategized on how best to deploy economic boycotts. The boycott was thus embedded in a much broader vision of emancipation that touched on all aspects of social and political life. As Qumsiyeh documents, there was a wide spectrum of boycott actions and acts of political refusal, including "strikes ... refusal to pay taxes, developing self-sufficiency through farming and other methods, mass resignations (from the police, municipal councils, and other authorities), ... refusal to obey military orders to close universities and schools (classes were held in people's homes, mosques, and churches, and even cellars and caves) ... flying the Palestinian flag (this was forbidden by military order)."[65] Palestinians even refused to set their clocks to Israeli daylight time, so that the boycott extended to time, and the temporality of colonization, as well.

These popular acts of resistance collectively represent a profound assertion of sovereignty, self-determination, and decolonization. As Ibrahim Dakkak eloquently observed, the Intifada was essentially a social revolution:

> The intifada was an intifada in the underlying construction of the Palestinian people in how people go about their daily lives. The intifada became a way of living and this is not covered in the media. The intifada was moving in the direction of building ... a Palestinian independence route. It means independence from Israeli markets, staying as far away as possible from Israeli institutions, building Palestinian institutions that are as independent as possible ... the intifada involves in [*sic*] daily confrontation with the occupation and also in reordering the elements of Palestinian society in light of what fits the situation.[66]

Dakkak's statement articulates a decolonial principle of cultural, in addition to political, liberation enacted through the withdrawal of collusion with colonial institutions; this, I argue, is at the core of the academic as well as cultural boycott of Israel.

A striking example of the assertion of Palestinian autonomy and self-governance expressed through boycott, under the brutal conditions of Israeli military occupation and colonial repression during the first Intifada, was the tax boycott in the West Bank town of Beit Sahour, adjacent to Bethlehem. In 1988, residents of Beit Sahour (as documented by Qumsiyeh, who is himself from the town) refused to pay taxes and about a thousand Palestinians even discarded their Israeli cards. Israel responded with a military curfew, invasion with tanks, raids of stores and homes, arrests without trial (what is euphemistically known as "administrative detention"), rubber bullets, and tear gas, as well as threats of deportation and punishment of Palestinians without ID cards. But as Qumsiyeh points out, this collective punishment was met with collective efforts by local residents to establish self-sufficiency, such as low-cost medical programs, an agricultural cooperative, and a clandestine dairy.

The legendary Beit Sahour boycott, and in particular the self-reliance project to boycott Israeli milk by smuggling eighteen cows into the West Bank, is the subject of the brilliant documentary film, *The Wanted 18.*[67] The cows were actually hunted down as fugitives by the Israeli military, and the Palestinian youth who were involved had to go into hiding; one young man from Beit Sahour was killed by soldiers in retaliation for his organizing. What is most inspiring about this moving film—which combines animation, interviews, and archival footage—is that it documents the ways Palestinians in Beit Sahour engaged in the "social" Intifada that Dakkak described above, imagining a Palestinian society that involved refusal of complicity with the colonial economy and regime, on the one hand, and a model of collectivity and autonomy, on the other. This movement upended social hierarchies of gender, generation, and class in order to work toward a vision of self-determination and equality. As one of the participants in the tax revolt, Makram Sa'ad, eloquently observed: "There were no leaders; everyone participated.... We were all Palestinians ... we suffered alike and protested alike."[68] This is not to romanticize the first Intifada but to point out how this statement echoes the narratives cited earlier about civil disobedience in the U.S civil rights struggle, especially the student sit-in movement in the South, which were indeed grassroots, collective efforts where leadership emerged from the bottom up.[69] It also gestures to the war of position and the revolutionary struggle to challenge the social order through cultural transformation. The political experiment in Beit Sahour powerfully encapsulates the dual thrust of the boycott: a politics of refusal, and a politics of decolonization and solidarity.

In the following chapter, I will discuss the calls for boycott by Palestinians that followed the first Intifada and culminated in the formation of the academic and cultural boycott movement in the United States, although this movement builds on the many acts of civil disobedience by Palestinians that preceded the emergence of what is called BDS today. Furthermore, the Palestinian boycott campaign is firmly situated in the history of the South African antiapartheid campaign—drawing inspiration from the deployment of boycott and divestment in that global solidarity movement as well as the break with Zionism that it spurred on the left—and it extends the genealogy of international solidarity as well as antiracist and labor organizing in the United States.

TWO

The Academic Boycott Movement

The U.S. academic boycott movement emerged as an organized force in the late 2000s, with the formation of USACBI (US Campaign for the Academic and Cultural Boycott of Israel) by scholar-activists with a shared commitment to the Palestinian freedom struggle.[1] It was during the war on Gaza in the winter of 2008–9 that a group of academics from different disciplines formed an official structure for building a national academic and cultural boycott movement and for recruiting U.S. academics to endorse the call by the Palestinian Campaign for the Academic and Cultural Boycott of Israel (PACBI).[2] In this chapter, I briefly chart the history of the academic boycott movement in the United States and academic boycott campaigns in different professional academic associations, drawing on interviews with key organizers from different fields and situating these campaigns in the context of deeper intellectual and political shifts associated with the ascendance of critical ethnic and race studies and the transnationalization of American studies. I begin with an account of the founding of the first national U.S. academic and cultural boycott campaign, an organization in which I have been involved as a founding member. I will show how the emergence of this campaign can be traced to the significant political realignment vis-à-vis Palestine-Israel that has occurred in the U.S. academy and in the public sphere in recent years.

USACBI: THE TIME IS *NOW*

The story of how USACBI was founded is an interesting one, as it reveals both the core tensions in the politics of BDS and Palestine-Israel in the academy, and also USACBI's development as a (boycott) movement organization. The founding scholar-activists all happened to be based in California, as they belonged to California Scholars for Academic Freedom (CS4AF), a network of (now over one hundred) academics created after 9/11 to challenge the censorship of scholars doing critical work in Middle East studies, particularly related to Palestine-Israel. As Israeli bombs rained down on the blockaded Gaza Strip in January 2009, destroying schools and universities in addition to homes and hospitals, and terrorizing the trapped local population, a discussion emerged on the network's listserv. How should we, as U.S. taxpayers indirectly sending financial support to Israel, express our solidarity with Palestinians who were enduring ongoing massacres, siege, and occupation? How could we as scholars condemn Israel's flouting of international human rights and its assaults on (Palestinian) human life?

Some of us were concerned that the discourse of academic freedom was not enough to address the lockdown on criticism of Israel in the academy, nor the urgent "facts on the ground" in Palestine-Israel. Among progressives in general there had been growing frustration with the United States' role as a powerful, unconditional ally of Israel, which receives more U.S. economic and military aid than any other country, whether from a Democratic or Republican administration (currently about $3 billion annually, or about $10 million in military aid per day).[3] Bill Mullen, professor of American studies at Purdue University and member of USACBI's organizing collective, reflects on the historical impetus for the academic boycott movement's formal emergence in the United States, in the wake of Barack Obama's election as president:

> I think it was the Israeli invasion of Gaza in December 2008 /January 2009. Obama had just been elected and there were a lot of young people—young people of color especially—excited about what his presidency might mean. Then he stood silently by during the bombings and slaughter of 1,500 Palestinians. At the same time, Western mass media images of dead and dying Palestinians saturated the internet and television. That moment "woke" a lot of people. It helped to show them that Obama, and the Democratic Party, were complicit in the Israeli Occupation. It expressed the real "face" of the Occupation as a brutally violent Zionist project. It also . . . created a wider public space for Palestinian and Arab intellectuals to speak to broader audiences about the Occupation.

In addition to the growing realization that even a liberal (or progressive) U.S. president would not condemn Israel's war crimes, an important moment for the BDS movement was when the president of the United Nations General Assembly, Father Miguel D'Escoto Brockmann, speaking at the United Nations' commemoration of the International Day of Solidarity with the Palestinian People in November 2008, made a passionate statement condemning the assault on Gaza and supporting self-determination for Palestine: "I believe that the failure to create a Palestinian State as promised is the single greatest failure in the history of the United Nations.... It has been 60 years since some 800,000 Palestinians were driven out of their homes and property, becoming refugees and an uprooted and marginalized people."[4] D'Escoto noted that it was soon to be the sixtieth anniversary of the adoption of the Universal Declaration of Human Rights, which enshrines the right to self-determination; in a remarkably eloquent statement, he said, "We are witness to decades of the terrible conditions endured throughout the occupied Palestinian territory, yet the promise—the right—of the Palestinian people to a homeland remains as elusive as ever."[5] The Nicaraguan official described this failure of human rights as a "bitter irony" and went further in condemning Israel's policy as a "version of the hideous policy of apartheid."[6] D'Escoto's speech was circulated widely, for not only did it depart from the diplomatic tone of most international leaders, but he actually called publicly for BDS actions targeting Israel. In essence, he argued that Palestinians have been an exception to human rights, their suffering not worthy of censure by many who denounce human rights abuses elsewhere—thus representing a particular contradiction of rights-talk that I will address later.

D'Escoto's passionate call for "concrete action" and BDS was shared on the CS4AF listserv, and a few of us suggested it was about time to respond to the 2004 call from Palestinian scholars and activists for an academic boycott of Israel, and to mobilize an official campaign. However, as with D'Escoto's statement, which prompted furious responses from Zionist groups, there was a tense discussion within the network. At the time, most responded by saying that the boycott was not strategic, that it was ineffective, untimely, and problematic, and they refused to endorse the PACBI call. This opposition was from scholars who were otherwise critical of Israel but who thought that the boycott would somehow harm the Palestine solidarity movement or that it was not the right time (again, when is it ever the *right* time?). Clearly, there were many underlying anxieties and fears of reprisals from Zionists, anxieties that were not unfounded. The network decided—rather ironically for a group concerned with academic freedom—that discussion of boycott would not be allowed on the list. However, boycott advocates immediately started reaching out to other scholars they knew would be supportive of an academic boycott beyond the network. We quickly launched a national campaign for academic and cultural boycott based on the principles of PACBI.

The circumstances in which USACBI was founded are significant because, first, it was formed out of a sense of urgency and without long years of planning, and second, it emerged from a battle over censorship. This explains both the early organizational history of the campaign and its central role in disrupting the permissible academic consensus related to Palestine and Zionism. We were in a position of challenging the acceptable parameters of Palestine solidarity among U.S. academics, which has been a central goal, and also outcome, of the academic boycott movement. All the founding members already had experience with academic repression in one form or another related to Palestine-Israel; there were also Palestinian scholars in this founding group. While the historical formation and membership of the founding group was rather serendipitous, and much work happened later to put in place an organizing structure as well as include members beyond California, from the outset USACBI provided a space for scholar-activists unafraid to step beyond sanctioned political discourse and the liberal-progressive status quo. In this sense, USACBI was and remains a radical interruption of academic politics related to Palestine-Israel. Since then, many scholars in CS4AF now support the academic boycott and advocate for it publicly. As with all political movements, the boundary of what is acceptable shifts over time. The academic boycott has continued to push the horizon of knowledge production about Palestine-Israel beyond what has been deemed "safe" for the U.S. academy.

USACBI's call for academic boycott was not in fact the first from U.S. academics. In 2002, a group of academics (including Mazin Qumsiyeh, Mona Baker, and several others) launched a petition for an academic boycott, collecting five hundred signatures, and formed Academics for Justice. Earlier calls for BDS had also come from Palestine, such as a statement by Palestinian civil society groups in August 2002, following the Durban World Conference on Racism.[7] But USACBI provided a national platform advocating for academic and cultural boycott, in line with PACBI's call, and a structure for endorsement by U.S. scholars and cultural workers. Zionists immediately took note of this new political development in the United States and declared that USACBI would represent a real threat to Israel only if it garnered five hundred signatures; initially, it was a small list of perhaps just over one hundred endorsers. Members of the organizing collective engaged in the arduous work of adding endorsements by academics (and artists) one by one, in the process having important educational conversations about Palestine and creating intellectual and political space.

The call to endorse USACBI is itself a starting point for critical political conversation about Palestine solidarity:

> PACBI and the entire movement for boycott, divestment, and sanctions (representing the overwhelming majority among Palestinian civil society parties, unions, networks and organizations) emphasize fundamental Palestinian rights, sanctioned by international

law and universal human rights principles that ought to be respected by Israel to end the boycott. We struggle to achieve an end to Israel's three-tiered injustice and oppression: 1) occupation and colonization in the 1967-occupied Palestinian territory; 2) denial of the refugees' rights, paramount among which is their right to return to their homes of origin, as per UN General Assembly Resolution 194; and 3) the system of racial discrimination, or apartheid, to which Palestinian (all non-Jewish) citizens of Israel are subjected to.

The principles guiding the PACBI campaign and the three goals outlined above are also points of unity for the US Campaign for the Academic and Cultural Boycott of Israel (USCACBI). We believe it is time to take a public, principled stance in support of equality, self-determination, human rights (including the right to education), and true democracy, especially in light of the censorship and silencing of the Palestine question in U.S. universities, as well as U.S. society at large. There can be no academic freedom in Israel/Palestine unless all academics are free and all students are free to pursue their academic desires.[8]

Thus, one of the key principles of USACBI's work is not just building a structure for Palestine solidarity in the academy especially, as well as for cultural workers and artists to some extent, but also enlarging *intellectual and political space* for critical discussion of Palestine-Israel. The mission statement is also clear that USACBI expands academic freedom—rather than diminishing it, as anti-BDS critics have claimed. I will discuss at greater length in Chapter 3 how USACBI has provided a collective space of public support and solidarity for U.S. academics daring to cross the red line and express support for Palestinian liberation.

At the time of its founding, USACBI's organizing collective included just a dozen scholars and activists, mostly based in California, though the advisory board has always had an impressive roster of internationally renowned intellectuals and activists, such as Archbishop Desmond Tutu, Ilan Pappe, Vijay Prashad, Bill Fletcher Jr., (the late) Adrienne Rich, Cornel West, Hamid Dabashi, Glen Ford, and Jasbir Puar, among several others.[9] Today, five years and two more wars on Gaza later, USACBI has over twelve hundred academic endorsers (and about five hundred endorsements from cultural workers) as well as an expanded organizing collective that includes scholars, students, and activists from across the United States. In fact, when the list of endorsers crossed five hundred in 2010, USACBI and the boycott movement began to register for Zionists in the United States and Israel as a "strategic threat" to Israel's legitimacy, as part of the growing BDS movement on college campuses around the country and globally. The academic and cultural boycott campaign works in tandem with divestment campaigns organized by undergraduate (and graduate) students, as part of the larger BDS movement that provides a guiding framework based on the three principles outlined earlier, and that offers a toolkit, or repertoire, of different tactics and strategies that can be deployed in various contexts. The adaptability and flexibility of the BDS framework is one of its key strengths and has helped fuel its success. USACBI has also provided a national platform for organizing, into which academics can plug in to mobilize at the grassroots level, and publicly, as well as collectively, express solidarity with Palestine.

ACADEMIC BOYCOTT ORGANIZING AND THE USACBI DELEGATION TO PALESTINE

The powerful force of the mass movement supporting BDS in the academy became visible in the historic academic boycott resolution endorsed by the American Studies Association (ASA) in December 2013.[10] A huge majority of ASA members who voted on the resolution supported the academic boycott of Israeli institutions in what became a stunning victory for the academic boycott movement in the United States. This was the moment when it became clear that the tide had turned in the academy. U.S. academics (and U.S. and Israeli political leaders) took note of the growing boycott movement and retaliated against the threat it represented to the status quo. But the ASA boycott resolution was actually not the first endorsed by a national academic association in the United States; it was preceded by the pioneering resolution adopted by the Association of Asian American Studies (AAAS) and unanimously endorsed by members present at its business meeting at the national conference in April 2013.[11] There was also a resolution supporting academic and cultural boycott by the Association for Humanist Sociology, a small organization that did not get much attention at the time.[12] In the following years, academic boycott resolutions were adopted by a host of other academic associations.[13]

How did these boycott campaigns emerge to challenge the powerful status quo in the academy? Was it a coincidence that these resolutions were passed by associations of ethnic and American studies (and not Middle East studies), and in interdisciplinary fields and not the traditional disciplines? Two interrelated phenomena explain the historic victories in the ASA and AAAS and their challenge to the dominant Zionist discourse that had long been the norm in the academy, despite—or perhaps even because of—its liberalism. One factor is the intellectual shifts, including the ascendance of critical ethnic, race, queer, and indigenous studies, that had occurred in American studies. These are all interdisciplinary fields and it is the interdisciplinarity of American studies that allowed for a basis for praxis and activism that is not generally possible in the more conservative disciplinary fields, such as English, history, or sociology. Related to the critical turn in the field is the greater focus in American and ethnic studies on the links between the United States and West Asia (the Middle East) since 9/11 and the growing critique both of U.S. imperialism in the global War on Terror, and of the repression of Arab and Muslim American communities. As the AAAS resolution noted in providing the context for solidarity with Palestine in Asian American studies: "Arab (West Asian) and Muslim American communities, students, and scholars have been subjected to profiling, surveillance, and civil rights violations that have circumscribed their freedom of political expression, particularly in relation to the issue of human rights in Palestine-Israel."[14] The Palestine question was thus acknowledged as central to the disciplining and regulation of Arab and Muslim Americans after 9/11, as well as to progressive solidarity and human rights activism. There was also an increasing transnationalization of ethnic (including Asian American) and American studies, accompanied by the emergence in Palestine studies of a settler colonial studies framework that linked the field to concerns with indigeneity in American and Native studies and provided an intellectual scaffolding for anticolonial and antiracist politics. These intellectual shifts are related to the generational shift that has led graduate students and junior scholars across disciplines to support the boycott, thus challenging the academic culture of a previous generation that pivoted on self-censorship and academic policing vis-à-vis Palestine-Israel.

The second factor to be noted in the rise of boycott organizing were the personal encounters of left scholars with Palestine, propelled by their commitments to international solidarity in the context of other political work they were doing. The leadership of the boycott campaigns mentioned above came from a diverse group of scholars, all of whom were members of the organizing collective and advisory board of USACBI, or its supporters. These campaigns in turn each created a foundation for organizing in other fields, creating an archive of knowledge and repertoire of strategies that activists could draw on in subsequent campaigns. For example, Cynthia Franklin, professor of English at the University of Hawai'i(UH)–Manoa, recalls that she became active in the BDS movement after returning from a trip to Palestine in 2013, which compelled her to become a member of USACBI's organizing collective and actively involved in the ASA boycott campaign.

Franklin reflects that her commitment to boycott activism was crystallized when Kehaulani Kauanui, a native Hawaiian scholar-activist who is a USACBI advisory board member, gave a talk at UH–Manoa in 2012 about her recent trip to Palestine as part of an academic delegation organized by USACBI. Kauanui's talk, Franklin recalls, helped her understand "how conditions in Palestine articulate with those in Hawai'i—another site of settler colonialism and occupation." As a scholar-activist concerned with issues of Hawaiian sovereignty and solidarity activism, Franklin "discovered that when it comes to Palestine, only with the greatest of difficulty can research not lead to political involvement." Franklin also observes that her Palestine solidarity activism deepened her scholarly research and vice versa. This is borne out by the fact that UH–Manoa's ethnic studies department became the first academic department in the United States to issue a public statement endorsing the academic boycott, when they announced their support of the ASA boycott resolution in October 2013.[15] I think it is not coincidental that an ethnic studies department in Hawai'i was the first to endorse the boycott, given the centrality of indigenous politics and movements challenging settler colonialism in Hawai'i and the increasing concern with Palestine and transnational solidarity in ethnic studies.

The USACBI delegation that Kauanui participated in comprised leading scholars in critical ethnic and American studies whose scholarship and activism gave them an important vantage point to understand conditions in Palestine. That delegation was a pivotal event in the development of the academic boycott campaign in the ASA, and therefore of the larger movement in the United States inspired by the ASA resolution. Along with Kauanui, Robin Kelley, Bill Mullen, Nikhil Pal Singh, and Neferti Tadiar traveled to Palestine in January 2012 at the invitation of USACBI and met with academics, students, activists, and community members in the West Bank, Jerusalem, and Israel.[16] The delegation raised funds for their own travel expenses, and there was no grant or any external funding for the trip. This underscores that the delegation participants were deeply invested in the trip as an act of solidarity, in light of the proliferation of delegations to Palestine since then and the ambivalence many Palestinians understandably have long felt about political tourism (or "occu-tourism"). In fact, the delegation members committed to write about their experiences on returning to the United States, and to help catalyze solidarity among U.S. academics. As Mullen reflected:

> It was my participation in a USACBI delegation to Palestine in December 2012 that galvanized my organizing work around BDS and Palestine. Witnessing the everyday violence and brutality of Palestinian daily life firsthand was a life-changing experience. We encountered racism and settler colonialism in their most raw forms. I was also moved and inspired by the indomitable will of Palestin-

ians living under occupation. Every one we met—students, artists, prison activists, refugees, writers—had an unflinching commitment to resisting the occupation. It was like nothing I had ever seen or even experienced in all my reading on Palestine, or any place for that matter.

The USACBI delegation was incredibly transformative and provided a political and intellectual paradigm for the academic boycott movement, as its members produced a dossier of essays published in the *Social Text* blog *Periscope* a few months later.[17] The delegation also published a collective statement in *Periscope* in July 2012, in which they shared their observations, noting how Israel's apparatus of control regulates every aspect of Palestinian life, including access to education.[18] The statement recorded numerous instances of "appalling violations of Palestinian human rights and dignity," including restrictions on freedom of movement, home demolitions, land confiscation, evictions, disruption of families and marriages, walling projects, and racial discrimination against Palestinian citizens of Israel; it analyzed these as part of a regime of settler colonialism that aims to conquer as much Palestinian territory as possible while minimizing the Palestinian population. The statement also offered a powerful report on the degradations of academic freedom experienced by Palestinian scholars and students:

> As members of an international community of scholars, cultural workers and activists we remain specially attuned to the role that knowledge production, dissemination and exchange plays in both upholding and challenging relations of unequal power. Palestinian scholars and students are routinely denied academic freedom by the state of Israel. Israel has consistently closed Palestinian universities under security pretexts; international and Palestinian scholars living abroad are denied visas for faculty appointments in the

occupied territories. Israel thwarts Palestinian research capacities by restricting imports of equipment necessary for teaching basic science and engineering. It is all but impossible for Gaza students to attend West Bank universities, or for scholars from Ramallah, Gaza City, and eastern Jerusalem to meet in the same room. Even Israeli scholars who dissent from state policy face marginalization and harassment. Most Israeli (as well as US) academic institutions have been either silent or complicit in the face of Palestinian scientific, educational, medical, social, and political suffocation. Many Israeli academic institutions are directly involved in violations of Palestinian human rights and international law—from expropriating Palestinian lands to providing demographic, sociological, medical, legal and scientific research in the service of Israel's apartheid policies.[19]

This observation counters the common charges by opponents that the academic boycott undermines academic freedom, when in fact the boycott aims to enlarge academic freedom—for the oppressed population. The delegation did not merely provide an account of Israel's assaults on the Palestinian right to education and academic freedom as well as forms of dispossession and displacement that they witnessed. It also recommended a course of action for U.S. academics, pointing out the ways settler colonial rule in Palestine-Israel intersected with forms of colonial and settler regimes elsewhere, including the United States:

> As was the case with the US removal of tribal nations, the US South under anti-Black "Jim Crow" laws or South Africa under apartheid, Palestine today is the measure of the meaning and value of human rights in our time. By challenging injustice there we challenge the ways in which both US and Israeli security policies have normalized military colonialism, mass incarceration and permanent war both domestically and around the world, from the Pacific Islands to the Indian Ocean. There can be no self-determination and no

human rights under conditions of occupation, colonialism, segregation, or discrimination on the basis of race, ethnicity, nationality or religion. We urge our academic colleagues to join us in endorsing USACBI and upholding the principles of BDS in solidarity with our Palestinian counterparts.[20]

The delegation's statement provided a core framework for the academic boycott movement. It articulates the principles of international solidarity and anticolonial and antiracist politics that undergirded these campaigns, and also the work of USACBI and BDS at large. Clearly, these scholars were arguing for a radical vision of rights-based politics, which drives the BDS movement and which I will return to in Chapter 4.

The boycott resolution was a direct outcome of the delegation's experience, as the participants all felt a sense of urgency about taking collective action on their return from Palestine. These scholars took the lead in the boycott campaign in ASA and were progressive-left intellectuals and scholars of color who made important connections between their own antiracist, antiwar, and anticapitalist activism and the Palestinian freedom struggle. For example, Robin Kelley, now on USACBI's advisory board, said in an interview about his experiences in Palestine-Israel that he "witnessed a level of racist violence that I hadn't even seen growing up as a black person here in the States ... I have to say, and I've been beat by the cops. The level of racist violence from the settlers is kind of astounding."[21] Kelley offered a profound reflection, in an essay for the *Periscope* dossier, on the visceral experience of racism during his visit to Palestine-Israel and on the normalization of apartheid:

> I was prepared to gather "facts." I was *not* prepared for Israel's extraordinary efforts at normalization, and the Palestinians obstinate refusal

to accept Israel's projected image of itself as a "normal" modern democracy. It is a strange thing to cross the highly militarized zone dividing Ramallah from East Jerusalem, and minutes later stroll around Hebrew University's Mount Scopus campus, with its state-of-the-art library and computer center, its lovely hilltop view, its Aroma Espresso Bar where students and faculty can read, chat, and simulate normal university life. The embattled Sheikh Jarrah neighborhood, a mere twenty-minutes by foot, feels like another country.... As more and more young Palestinians create a democratic alternative to settler colonialism and its racist, anti-democratic ideology, and more people around the globe join the Boycott, Divestment, Sanctions movement and refuse to invest in Israel's regime of occupation and apartheid, the "government of injustice" will indeed vanish. And something beautiful will take its place.[22]

Using the jarring dissonance of the Israeli university adjoining an encaged and surveilled Palestinian population as an example of the contradictions of living under a settler colonial occupation, and in what could be called academic apartheid, Kelley argued eloquently for BDS as an expression of solidarity with grassroots, anticolonial resistance in Palestine. In his interview, he expressed the antiracist, transnational solidarity and anticolonial, left politics that are key to the academic boycott movement: "What we came away with is recognizing that this is a kind of joint, collective venture—that we are not advocating on behalf of Palestinians, but [are] partners with Palestinians for the right to self-determination. And the leadership comes from the Palestinian people. So we're supporting that movement, and recognizing that what's happening there is not exceptional, but rather part of a larger global process of late colonialism and neo-liberalism, and that what happens in Palestine is going to have an impact on the rest of the world."[23] The principle of self-determination is core to the academic boycott as articulated by Kelley, among others, and is key to understanding that the boycott, ultimately, is an act of solidarity with the Palestinian people's struggle for national liberation, and that it is not a replacement of that struggle.

Kauanui wrote about the meaning of the academic boycott for Palestinian academics inside the 1948 borders of Israel (those who belong to the community of '48 Palestinians) whom she met on her visit, and who pointed out to her that they were opposing not just occupation in the West Bank and Gaza, but the settler colonial project that Israel fundamentally represents, thus challenging the "deliberate partitioning" of Palestine. Kauanui was able to draw important connections to her own critique of settler governance in Hawai'i:

> What emerged from the conversation was that '48 Palestinians are attempting to shift the discourse to the paradigm of settler colonialism emerging from their concern with the general framework of discourse around the Palestinian question. This approach to boycott insists on a reframing to open up connections with all Palestinians. I could relate to this. In my work fighting the US occupation of Hawai'i, I routinely challenge the US government's legal claim to Hawai'i, expose the roots of the US as a settler colonial state, and critically engage the history of US imperialism in Native America and the Pacific Islands, insisting on the recognition of US empire as a form of violent, global domination.[24]

The academic boycott resolution in the ASA thus built on these analyses of critical race and indigenous studies scholars in American studies and on their critiques of racial supremacy and settler colonialism, providing a radical political framework that included but also extended BDS principles.

THE ASA BOYCOTT CAMPAIGN:
THE TURNING TIDE

The boycott campaign that was spurred by organizing done by USACBI delegation members helped revive and strengthen a politics of left internationalism in the ASA, and also in the AAAS and other academic organizations. Jordy Rosenberg, a member of USACBI's organizing collective and professor of English at the University of Massachusetts–Amherst, reflects on how they were drawn to the boycott movement because of the left internationalism it represented:

> I am reminded of a talk [USACBI collective member] Fred Moten gave in 2009 at the American Studies Association in which he conveys his gratitude for the Palestinian call for boycott. As Moten describes it, the call enables forms of collective solidarity from locations that, although at a physical remove from Palestine, experience a "refreshment" of radicalism through participating in an international, anticolonial movement.... I, too, am grateful for having found the boycott movement, and for the opportunity to be a part of it.... I became active in Palestine solidarity work in 2005, and, through that, I developed a sense of the vital internationalism that Fred speaks of.

Rosenberg was also involved in organizing around the resolution in the ASA, which did indeed reinvigorate radical academic activism among American studies scholars, as it was the campaign that has perhaps most vigorously engendered political debate in the association in recent years.

The delegation members submitted an academic boycott resolution through the Academic and Community Activism Caucus of the ASA, of which I was a cochair at the time with Malini Johar Schuller. The resolution was based on the guidelines of PACBI and called specifically for a boycott of Israeli academic institutions, *not* individuals, and for the right to speak openly about Palestine-Israel as scholars in American studies. At the fall 2012 annual meeting of the ASA, held in Puerto Rico, the Caucus set up a table next to the registration area to collect signatures in support of the resolution. It was incredible to witness the outpouring of public endorsement as academic after academic came up to sign the petition. The conference took place during the Israeli war on Gaza in 2012, in which over one hundred Palestinians were killed and during which the United States supported Israel, yet again. The very real context of asymmetrical warfare, of life and death, hovered over our boycott table, as scholars expressed outrage and also hopelessness about this latest attack on the Palestinian population trapped in the besieged Gaza Strip, whose air, land, and sea borders are still controlled by Israel. At the conference, the Caucus also organized a forum to discuss the boycott resolution, in a packed room where ASA members expressed overwhelming support for the academic boycott and volunteered to help in various ways. It was becoming clear to us that in fact there was more solidarity with Palestine and openness to the boycott than we had realized, but it was still not clear how much opposition by Zionists or others existed within the ASA.

This was not the first boycott resolution that was submitted to the ASA. The first was drafted by Marcy Newman, an anti-Zionist Jewish American scholar and founding member of USACBI, who had spent several years teaching at Palestinian universities. It was submitted directly to the executive committee after a meeting at the ASA in Oakland in 2006, in the wake of the Israeli war on Lebanon and Gaza. At the time, however, there was no BDS organizing in the ASA and this resolution predated the formation of USACBI as a national campaign. It was also a moment when the Zionist consensus was still the status quo in the U.S. academy, if crumbling on the peripheries, and solidarity with Palestine was marginalized and tenuous. An academic boycott was considered practically unthinkable. So the resolution was dismissed, but in subsequent years conversations continued among activist-scholars at the annual conference about organizing a boycott resolution. Several panels related to Palestine were also held at the ASA during these years, organized by USACBI members such as Newman and David Lloyd, another founding member of USACBI, and featuring speakers from Palestine. Scholars doing critical work on Palestine-Israel in transnational American studies were increasingly finding a receptive space in the ASA. This is also by way of pointing out that the antiboycott lobby's later allegation that the resolution was sprung on the ASA, supposedly by a secretive group of conspiring academics, is absurdly false. It emerged from ongoing public discussion in the ASA and after years of continuous organizing and increasing knowledge about BDS and PACBI, building on the national work of USACBI.

If anything, in the case of the ASA's academic boycott resolution, there was an excess of democratic process and collective decision making. After being submitted to the association's executive committee, per the organization's protocol, the resolution was tabled for a vote by the national council, an elected body of the ASA, at the fall meeting held in Washington, DC, in November 2013. The ASA hosted a town hall meeting at the conference on November 22 in which well-known American studies scholars discussed the context for the boycott; the meeting featured Steven Salaita, Kehaulani Kauanui, Angela Davis, Jasbir Puar, and Alex Lubin.[25] The executive committee also organized an open forum in a large auditorium on November 23 for members to openly discuss the resolution at the conference. This was also a first for an ASA resolution, and it was an opportunity to give all members present an opportunity to share their views publicly. Curtis Marez, professor of ethnic studies at UC San Diego, who was president of the ASA at the time, reflects on the outpouring of support for the resolution at the forum:

> When the ASA took its vote we really had no idea how it would turn out, so for me it was an important moment. If I had to further pinpoint an important turn of events it would be the public forum on the resolution at the ASA convention in 2013. My memory is that about one thousand people were there and to accommodate speakers we drew slips from a hat. A handful of people spoke in opposition but the majority spoke in powerful and moving terms in favor—from graduate students to very senior scholars in the field.

I was at the forum myself and I remember being completely unsure what would happen, steeling myself for the Zionist attacks and diatribes and possible protests that I had become accustomed to over the years at events about Palestine-Israel. The atmosphere in the large auditorium was electric as conference participants started lining up in the center of the hall to wait for a turn to speak. The executive committee members sat near a podium at the front of the room, and one of them pulled out numbered slips for speakers from the audience. As I stood at the back of the packed hall, I heard one speaker after another proclaiming support for the resolution and calling passionately for a boycott of Israeli academic institutions—to loud applause. I had goose bumps listening to this flood of declarations by faculty and students. The few speakers against the boycott, who made a pitiful case in defense of Israel, were vastly outnumbered. When I realized we had won the day, I was incredulous. The tide had turned.

The resolution, and the public forum, had given us an opportunity to materialize the silent support for the boycott and for Palestine that had been growing in recent years. The people who spoke from the floor, most of whom I did not know personally, already knew about the academic boycott and BDS movement; it was clear they were well informed and that the movement had spread like wildfire. This is what is so powerful about the academic boycott as a political instrument: it provides an opportunity for academics and students to take a position and to express collective solidarity. Rosenberg, who was also present that evening, recalls:

> I have a wonderful and powerful memory of being at the Open Forum on the BDS resolution at the American Studies Association meeting in 2013.... I remember those of us who were organizing toward the resolution had come prepared to speak in favor, in case no one else felt comfortable speaking in public on such a heavily censored and policed topic. I was waiting with my crumpled page of notes, ready to speak, when I realized that there would be no need. Person after person was coming up and speaking passionately and eloquently in favor of the resolution. That feeling of being sidelined as an organizer—of realizing you were surrounded by a large group of people with whom, unbeknownst to you, you were in solidarity—was truly beautiful and overwhelming. Tenured people, untenured people, graduate students, colleagues in contract and adjunct positions, all spoke with great courage and conviction. That moment of seeing how our collective commitment could create a space for truly free speech was unique and deeply powerful.

As Mullen described his account of USACBI's significance in the previous chapter, the academic boycott had become a mass movement. Marez and Rosenberg both use the word "powerful" in their reflections to describe that pivotal event at the ASA conference in DC, an event that was taken note of in the media as well. The boycott campaign was indeed a manifestation of that old-fashioned notion, people power. It was astonishing that there were so many contingent and untenured faculty, and even graduate students—the most precarious classes in the academy—who were willing to put themselves on the line to declare their solidarity with the Palestinian people in public. It was also clear that there had been a deepening pedagogy of BDS over the past few years. The boycott campaign created a space for supporters to emerge above ground, to show their collective force.

It was also striking to see the racial, ethnic, and sexual diversity of speakers in support of the boycott, and the homogeneity of those against it. On one side—as was to be the case in subsequent writing and organizing about the academic boycott—were scholars of color, queers, immigrants, indigenous people, and students. On the other side were White, generally older and very senior, academics, several in positions of institutional power and privilege. Lloyd, a USACBI organizer and founding member, reflected after the ASA forum on the intellectual and political shifts in American studies tied to the growing solidarity with Palestine:

Out of 44 speakers, whose names were submitted in writing and then drawn at random from a box, 37 spoke in favor of the boycott. They ranged from senior professors to graduate students and even undergraduate members of the association. All recalled the association's fundamental commitment to the study and critique of racism and the US histories of imperialism and settler colonialism.

Many made the connection between Israel as a settler colony and US complicity in politically and materially supporting its colonial projects. In doing so, several remarked that they were members of the association because its commitment to anti-racist and anti-colonial scholarship made it especially hospitable to their work. For them, the connection was self-evident between anti-racist work within the United States and solidarity work with the victims of a settler colonial project that has the fullest support of the United States.[26]

Echoing this view, Alex Lubin, an American studies scholar at the University of New Mexico in Albuquerque, who was one of the cofounders of the ASA's Activism Caucus (and at the time was director of the Center for American Studies and Research, at the American University of Beirut), also observed that support for the academic boycott was rooted in the "longer history of scholarly transformation within the ASA." He reflected on how the turn to settler colonial studies within American studies provided a foundation for anticolonial solidarity with Palestine: "Native American and indigenous studies scholars have always been active within Palestinian solidarity circles, but the recent growth of settler-colonial studies has provided the intellectual scaffolding through which to better understand settler-colonialisms rooted in liberal nation-states. Moreover, studies of settler-colonialism and indigeneity have allowed scholars to make comparison across time and space that bring into focus transnational processes of colonialism, as well as make evident new forms of anti-colonial solidarities. Recently, for example, Palestinian activists joined Idle No More, a global protest movement in support of indigenous rights."[27]

Significantly, a similar turn to settler colonial studies has also occurred in recent years in Palestine studies, rather belatedly, as that field has also shaken off some of the shackles of Zionist dominance and a new generation of critical Palestine studies and Palestinian and Arab scholars has engaged in comparative, global discussions of settler coloniality.[28] As Franklin and Rosenberg noted earlier, the turn to transnational American studies and a greater focus on indigenous studies provided a critical lens through which to engage with Palestine as a concern vital, not peripheral, to American studies. Accompanying this intellectual shift was the demographic and intellectual transformation of the leadership and membership of the ASA. In fact, the national council of the ASA comprised a highly diverse group of scholars that included faculty and graduate students from critical ethnic, feminist and queer, and indigenous studies, many of them scholars of color.

At a special session of the national council at the conference, members voted unanimously after much deliberation to endorse the boycott resolution. In an unprecedented move, they also decided to put a revised version of the resolution to a vote of the *entire* association with an online ballot after the conference, to ensure that members had a chance to collectively express their views on the boycott, and cognizant of the charged nature of BDS in the academy. I was a member of the national council at the time (as was Kauanui), and the group worked round the clock on e-mail for a week after the ASA meeting to collectively produce the revised resolution. On December 16, in an online election that attracted 1,252 voters—the largest turnout for a ballot in the ASA's history—66 percent of voters endorsed the boycott resolution, while 30 percent voted against it. This overwhelming victory underscored the sea change that had occurred in the previous years on the Palestine question among U.S. academics, and in the United States at large.[29]

The ASA's adoption of the boycott was an astounding moment, with national and global reverberations as political leaders in both the United States and Israel took note of the resolution. David Palumbo-Liu, professor of comparative literature at Stanford who was an active supporter of both the AAAS and

ASA boycott resolutions, and current USACBI organizing collective member, reflected on the resolutions:

> I was at the ASA town hall in Washington, DC, and the last word at the panel was from Angela Davis. She ended her statement with something like, "We have to catch up with the AAAS on this issue." I went down afterwards to thank her, and to say many in the AAAS felt exposed and vulnerable after the vote to boycott, and her words meant a lot. It was that moment of solidarity that was inspiring, and it has only grown since, and exponentially so. The transition from a resolution passed by a relatively small, ethnic-specific academic organization, to one passed by an exponentially larger organization with a much longer history, was highly significant.

When the ASA passed its resolution, it made the front page of the *New York Times*. Palumbo-Liu also notes that these boycott resolutions marked the growing significance of the U.S. academy in challenging the censorship of the Palestine question, pointing out that that is precisely what was so threatening to the political establishment:

> The taboo regarding even talking about Israel in a seriously critical manner has been lifted. People are no longer feeling nearly as alone and isolated when they do. They have a huge national and international movement as a backdrop. It is absolutely critical to note that this change did not come from mainstream politics. Nor simply the grass roots. The prominence of Palestine in political debate today came from the academy, precisely the place we were used to thinking was a dead zone for politics since the Reagan-Thatcher neoliberal hegemony kicked in. Now every action by religious, labor, or other groups to divest is seen as part of a larger movement that includes the academy.

Edward Said had noted many years ago that Palestine was the "last taboo" in the U.S. public sphere; finally, the taboo had been broken.[30] There was a sense of collective exhilaration after the

ASA vote was announced and a feeling of having broken through what had been viewed as an insurmountable barricade. It was also a moment, as Palumbo-Liu notes, of revived academic activism driven partly by BDS organizing.

The ASA resolution that was adopted explicitly linked its support for the academic boycott to the enlargement of academic freedom and commitment to antiracism, stating:

> Whereas the American Studies Association is committed to the pursuit of social justice, to the struggle against all forms of racism, including anti-Semitism, discrimination, and xenophobia, and to solidarity with aggrieved peoples in the United States and in the world; ...

> Whereas the American Studies Association is dedicated to the right of students and scholars to pursue education and research without undue state interference, repression, and military violence, and in keeping with the spirit of its previous statements supports the right of students and scholars to intellectual freedom and to political dissent as citizens and scholars;

> It is resolved that the American Studies Association (ASA) endorses and will honor the call of Palestinian civil society for a boycott of Israeli academic institutions. It is also resolved that the ASA supports the protected rights of students and scholars everywhere to engage in research and public speaking about Israel-Palestine and in support of the boycott, divestment, and sanctions (BDS) movement.[31]

The ASA resolution also articulated its solidarity with Palestinian students and scholars whose academic freedom has been degraded, and pointed to the role of the United States in enabling violations of the right to education in Palestine:

> Whereas the United States plays a significant role in enabling the Israeli occupation of Palestine and the expansion of illegal settlements and the Wall in violation of international law, as well as in supporting

the systematic discrimination against Palestinians, which has had documented devastating impact on the overall well-being, the exercise of political and human rights, the freedom of movement, and the educational opportunities of Palestinians;

Whereas there is no effective or substantive academic freedom for Palestinian students and scholars under conditions of Israeli occupation, and Israeli institutions of higher learning are a party to Israeli state policies that violate human rights and negatively impact the working conditions of Palestinian scholars and students;[32]

This statement framing the boycott as *for* academic freedom clearly articulates that the problem of academic freedom is most acute for Palestinian scholars and students (one in which the United States is complicit via its support for Israel); that is, there is a racialized differential in access to academic freedom. U.S. scholars based in the global North are privileged and also complicit in the assaults on academic, and human, freedom in Palestine. As Lloyd and Schuller point out:

The censorship that US academics and citizens face regarding criticism of Israel is negligible compared to the daily regime of occupation and siege that denies Palestinian scholars the right to free movement and prevents them from attending classes, taking exams, or studying abroad on fellowship; that subjects universities to frequent and arbitrary closures that constitute collective punishment; or that willfully destroys academic institutions, such as the American International School and the Islamic University of Gaza, which were destroyed in 2009 along with some twenty other schools and colleges. If there has been anywhere a systematic denial of academic freedom to a whole population, rather than to specific individuals or to institutions, it is surely in Palestine under Israeli occupation.[33]

Lloyd and Schuller also analyze this degradation of Palestinian academic freedom as a strategy of settler colonialism, for they observe that "Palestinian education, like Palestinian culture and civil society, has been systematically targeted for destruction" by the powerful Israeli colonial regime.[34] So the boycott is fundamentally an act of transnational, anticolonial, and antiracist solidarity.

The ASA boycott resolution immediately provoked responses from American studies departments, other professional academic associations, and university administrators, as well as politicians, who condemned it, attacked the ASA, and in some cases withdrew their membership. I will discuss the opposition to the ASA and academic boycott in the following chapter, but here I note that while there was a strong backlash, the 2013 vote in the ASA also spurred boycott campaigns in several other (mainly interdisciplinary) associations. It was followed by boycott resolutions adopted by the African Literature Association, Critical Ethnic Studies Association, Native American and Indigenous Studies Association, Peace and Justice Studies Association, Native American Studies Association, and the National Association of Chicana and Chicano Studies, among others.[35] Petitions in support of the boycott also erupted in fields whose associations did not officially adopt the boycott or resisted doing so despite their members' advocacy, such as a statement by over four hundred prominent scholars in Middle East studies in 2014. Also, in December 2014, the UC graduate student workers union, UAW Local 2865, became the first mainstream labor union to officially endorse BDS and call for divestment, in a vote in which 52 percent of members endorsed an individual pledge to support the academic boycott.[36] In 2016, boycott and BDS resolutions were also adopted, respectively, by the CUNY Doctoral Students' Council and by UAW Local 2110's Graduate Student Organizing Committee (GSOC) at New York University (where a majority of GSOC voters pledged to support the academic boycott)—the first private university union to support BDS.

The major boycott campaigns inspired by the ASA that have particularly shaken up the U.S. academy, though they have not yet been successful, have been those in the Modern Language Association (MLA) and the American Anthropological Association (AAA). These represent major disciplines (the ASA and AAAS are smaller associations representing interdisciplinary fields), and the campaigns have extended over long periods of time. Lisa Rofel, professor of anthropology at UC Santa Cruz, recalls how the AAA boycott campaign began with grassroots mobilizing by academics, similar to that in the ASA: "The first year, we just stood in the lobby of the American Anthropology Association meetings and collected signatures! Very presocial media tactics! We also had a panel discussion of the Israeli occupation. Since the response was overwhelmingly positive, we formed a group to work on a boycott resolution. This group has been ... a real mixture of people by generation, gender, ethnicities, and sexualities, of Palestinians, Israelis, Americans, and Europeans."

In December 2015, after months of organizing and public discussion on social media as well as at the conference, AAA members voted in favor of holding a referendum on the boycott by a massive majority of 88 percent. In the spring of 2016 there was an online ballot and the resolution was defeated by "a razor-thin margin of 39 votes, 2,423–2,384 (50.4%–49.6%)."[37] As one of the AAA boycott campaign's organizers noted about the vote, however, the campaign had already been successful in creating space for critical discussion of Palestine-Israel in anthropology: "Even setbacks like the AAA loss are not just 'losses' but moments during which the conversation continues to move forward, new spaces for teaching people about the realities of the Israeli state oppression are opened, etc." As this anthropologist and boycott organizer also observes, "I think the boycott movement will continue its work. The point is not the boycott; the point is to use boycott as a means/pressure point to an end. Boycott is a tool; it is not the end goal." In the MLA, a boycott campaign spearheaded by several USACBI organizers submitted a resolution in 2015, but the vote was postponed till the 2017 MLA conference, where it was defeated by a relatively slim margin in the delegate assembly (concurrently, an antiboycott resolution narrowly passed).

This reframing of what "success" or "failure" means in the academic boycott movement is crucial: the goal of the boycott movement is not just winning votes in resolutions per se; it is about the victory that occurs in the *process* of organizing for a vote that forces scholars and students to engage in critical and public discussion about Palestine, Israeli occupation, apartheid, settler colonization, Zionism, and U.S. imperialism. The end game of the boycott is not (just) about the vote, even if this is an important component of collective, democratic decision making among academics. The end game is winning intellectual, and political, space. In this sense, the boycott movement is waging a Gramscian war of position, not just a war of maneuver.

CONCLUSION

In every instance, whether in the AAAS or the AAA, boycott campaigns have reinvigorated academic activism and provided a hub for left scholars to organize. Given the increasing professionalization of academics working in neoliberal university spaces that undermine collectivity and discourage "risky" scholarship or political engagement, this impact of the boycott is extremely significant. For example, Lubin reflected on how the

ASA boycott campaign reenergized left activism and transnational solidarity among scholars beyond U.S. borders:[38]

> I have studied global solidarity movements, but this was the first time that I felt what it was like to be part of one. Throughout the conference I received e-mails from friends in Beirut and Cairo, as well as from scholars across the US who lent their support and wanted to know what was happening at the conference. Moreover, those of us involved in the boycott movement saw evidence of how our scholarship informs all aspects of our lives, including our activism. The boycott supporters brought to our activism scholarly knowledge about social movements in the past and present that we could draw on for comparison and for inspiration. Whether it was by contributing their insights about the United Farm Workers struggle, the indigenous struggle for sovereignty, the prison abolition movement or the South African anti-apartheid movement, scholar activists put ideas into action in ways that were both inspiring and revelatory.

Echoing this observation of global, cross-racial solidarity, Rofel pointed out that the Ferguson-Palestine solidarity movement also "made a significant difference in our organizing within Anthropology," as the Black Lives Matter movement that erupted at the time also galvanized African American anthropologists and antiracist allies within the AAA. The Ferguson 2 Gaza campaign provoked important discussions about U.S.-Israeli collaboration in policing, surveillance, and militarization, as did the Dream Defenders delegations of Black activists to Palestine. As the Dream Defenders state, "DD Palestine is part of the resurgence of internationalism within the US-based movements for justice, especially inspired by the connections of Black and Palestinian liberation."[39] BDS has become one node, and an important and dynamic one, in these transnational coalitions and cross-racial solidarity movements.

The academic boycott movement is itself embedded in a social movement and is part of a growing grassroots mobilization that involves progressive-left academics, students, union organizers, indigenous activists, human rights advocates, Black radicals, and Palestinian, Arab, and Muslim communities and their allies, including Jewish American solidarity activists. This social movement has expanded in large part due to the flourishing of campus activism by students, and the expansion of Students for Justice in Palestine (SJP) groups across the United States. SJP, founded in 2001, is a multiracial solidarity movement, not based on ethnic/religious identity, that has spawned autonomous chapters on campuses across the United States that have led BDS campaigns.[40] Divestment campaigns spearheaded by SJP chapters and similar student groups have proliferated, forming cross-racial coalitions and alliances with other social justice groups, and have helped politicize students as well as faculty. They have provided a context for educating otherwise woefully underinformed U.S. students about Middle East politics and U.S. foreign policy. I have found in my own research on Arab and Muslim American student activism after 9/11 that the Israeli assault on Gaza in the winter of 2008–9 was a turning point in the political involvement of young people who became galvanized to participate in antiwar and Palestine activism at the same moment that academics were compelled to launch USACBI and the academic boycott movement.[41]

The BDS movement has also become a venue for Palestinian student leadership in a new generation of Palestinian Americans that has helped make Palestine solidarity one of the most important social justice movements on university campuses. Lena Ibrahim, who was an SJP activist in the Washington, DC, area and also part of USACBI's organizing collective, wrote about how she was inspired by her involvement with the ASA campaign. Her experience demonstrates how undergraduate students are increasingly connected to the academic boycott movement, not just divestment campaigns, and are forging alliances with progressive-left faculty through this movement. Ibrahim thoughtfully reflected on why her involvement in the ASA boycott campaign and participation at the 2013 conference was so transformative for her as a Palestinian American student: "I, as a student, was completely in shock. I met some of the most incredible professors who not only supported the Palestinian cause, but were eager in wanting to share their outspoken support. I spoke with professors and scholars from all around the country who wanted me to know they were working hard on their campuses to empower SJP students like myself and to finally break the deliberately set up barrier in discussion on Palestine/Israel in academia."[42] For Ibrahim, having grown up in a society in which Palestinian identity is often suppressed or erased, including in the academy, the recognition of Palestine as a cause for global justice and solidarity was personally, as well as politically, meaningful. She said eloquently of the ASA open forum:

> It was historic because every second I stood at the 2013 ASA conference I thought of every single activist I knew, every single Palestinian I knew, and I wished that they could be standing right next to me witnessing it. I wanted those people next to me because I knew what I was feeling was an empowerment that we very rarely feel in this particular setting. A setting I now realize is crucial for activism work and Palestinian solidarity alike. It was historic because now as I sit to try and write what happened at ASA, I struggle, as words just can't do it justice.
>
> It's always a controversial thing to talk about being Palestinian, even more controversial to talk about Palestinian solidarity activism, in most American settings, especially an academic one. This

has always seemed strange to me because academia is a place for trusted study, for trusted truths, not a place where social issues can somehow find a way to escape criticism and unrestricted discussion, the way Israel has overwhelmingly been able to do in American academia which has directly distorted the Palestinian narrative and its related activism in the US. The 2013 American Studies Association not only challenged this notion, but completely crushed it, as it gave an undergraduate student like myself enough inspiration to last me until well after graduation.[43]

Ibrahim's personal reflections highlight the ways BDS campaigns and organizing in the academy have helped counter the exceptionalist repression of Palestinian narratives, and she echoes the accounts of other Palestinian American youth and students. An important cultural and racial politics is thus at work here for groups who are made invisible, censored, and subjugated due to the collusion of the United States with Israel and the ways this "special relationship" has filtered into and been bolstered by the U.S. academy.

SJP students and Palestine solidarity activists are accustomed to dealing with repression and backlash, and many of us had steeled ourselves for the attacks on the ASA that unfolded after the vote. Rajini Srikanth, who helped lead the boycott campaign in the AAAS and was involved in the MLA resolution, notes that the growing strength of the boycott movement has been accompanied by an increasingly ferocious counter-campaign:

> The intensity of the vilification campaign is perhaps a measure of the success of BDS efforts in the United States—with several academic organizations having passed or considering the academic boycott resolution, trade unions voting in support of BDS, student groups forcing divestment of university funds from companies benefitting from the Occupation.... Senior university administrators have almost unanimously denounced the academic boycott as

a threat to academic freedom, but this position merely underscores the power structures within the US academy and their mirroring of the US government's uncritical and unconditional support of Israel and its policies. Nonetheless, the academic boycott movement has opened up discursive space to talk about Israel's policies; this is a very salutary development.

In the following chapter, I address the antiboycott campaign that has attempted to counter the growing strength of the BDS movement through tactics of vilification, censorship, harassment, and lawfare, as Srikanth notes. Yet framing BDS as a social movement that has challenged powerful, hegemonic forces allows us to understand the responses by university administrations, corporate interests, and state and legislative bodies as a mapping of the power relations and alliances that are arrayed against BDS and that it has helped expose. Further, I will discuss how the backlash campaign is also a revealing site of knowledge about the connections between Zionism, U.S. imperialism, and neoliberal higher education that the boycott movement has successfully challenged.

THREE

Backlash

The Boycott and the Culture/Race Wars

It seems that nearly every conversation about the academic boy-cott inevitably touches on the backlash against it. There have indeed been ferocious, well-funded, and highly orchestrated campaigns opposing the boycott and BDS, relying on strategies of defamation, intimidation, and lawfare. Yet it is important to go beyond existing reports about the backlash, which has been well documented by now, and defenses of the boycott move-ment, and conceptualize this as an *archive of repression*.

In this chapter, I theorize the backlash by situating it in rela-tion to the culture wars, a site that illuminates the larger cul-tural politics in which the boycott is embedded. What is needed is an analysis of what this countermovement represents and the cultural and racial politics it has brought into view. I will exam-ine the anxieties about the boycott as revealing the political paradigm at the heart of the academic boycott, and as a lens into the racial and class wars in the U.S. academy. Attempts to sup-press the boycott movement shed light on the racial, class, gen-der, sexual, and national-colonial politics at the nexus of Zionist settler colonialism and U.S. imperialism. I argue that the rhetoric and tactics that constitute the backlash are components of an epistemology of Zionism that the academic boycott and BDS movements ultimately help produce.

THE WAR OF LEGITIMACY

The ferocity of the backlash against the BDS movement pivots on a core issue: the legitimacy of the Israeli state's policies toward the Palestinians and the threat to that legitimization that BDS represents. The war of legitimacy and counter-normalization matters a great deal to Israel. Israeli politicians have been increasingly worried by the damage done to Israel's public image in the international community; for example, it has tied with North Korea in global public opinion polls.[1] Its defenders have gone so far as to describe BDS and "delegitimization campaigns" as a "strategic threat with potentially existential implications" for Israel.[2] The backlash against the academic boycott and BDS more generally has been waged by a network of Zionist and right-wing organizations who defend those policies and by state legislatures and university administrators who uphold their legitimacy. The counter-boycott movement has been funded and supported by the Israeli government, which publicly announced that it has created programs to combat the growing influence of the BDS movement, through propaganda efforts known as *hasbara*, to counter the growing criticism of Israel, including in the United States, and by a well-funded "Brand Israel" campaign, which was launched in 2006—but which has existed unofficially for some years previously.[3] This rebranding effort spearheaded by the Israeli political leadership and organized in conjunction with Jewish Zionist organizations worldwide attempts to counter Israel's "delegitimization" through a massive, well-funded public relations campaign, relying on arts and cultural events, science and technology, and a coordinated, offensive strategy to discredit and counter BDS activism targeting universities.[4]

Zionist organizations such as the Reut Institute, a prominent Israeli think tank, have long claimed publicly that BDS and the boycott are a strategic, if not existential, threat to Israel and have developed strategies to defame and suppress the movement.[5] Omar Barghouti, the cofounder of PACBI, observed in 2015 that "Israel may soon be reaching its South Africa moment," citing influential Zionist Israeli leaders, such as Ehud Barak and the former Mossad chief, Shabtai Shavit, who expressed deep worries about "the future of the Zionist project" due to a "critical mass of threats," including the growing BDS movement. Shavit specifically noted the importance of the academy and deplored, "We are losing the fight for support for Israel in the academic world."[6] Barghouti comments, "Few forms of pressure have triggered as much alarm in Israel's establishment as the growing divestment movement on college campuses and the mushrooming support for academic boycott of Israel among US academic associations."[7] The academic boycott has also spread to other countries, such as India, in Europe, and most notably South Africa, where the University of Johannesburg became the first academic institution to sever its ties with an Israeli university, Ben Gurion University, in 2011.[8] This is significant because, as Barghouti notes, "Israel's academic institutions have, after all, been one of the pillars of Israel's regime of oppression, playing a major role in planning, implementing, justifying, and whitewashing Israel's crimes against the Palestinian people."[9]

The allegation that the boycott poses an "existential" or strategic threat to Israel implicitly acknowledges that Israel would be seriously challenged or even cease to exist by an attempt to make it a democratic state based on racial equality. The boycott and BDS fundamentally reframe the discourse about Israel and Zionism as its founding ideology. This explains the seriousness of the counter-boycott offensive. In 2015, Israeli prime minister Benjamin Netanyahu announced that the Israeli Ministry of Strategic Affairs and Information would receive at least 100 million Israeli shekels, as well as ten employees, solely to fight back against the BDS movement, as part of its mandate.[10] Netanyahu proclaimed at an emergency meeting in Las Vegas hosted by Republican billionaire and casino magnate Sheldon Adelson (the largest donor to Donald Trump's presidential campaign): "Delegitimization must be fought, and you are on the front lines." Israel approaches the BDS movement through the language and metaphor of war, recognizing that legitimacy is an important component of warfare for nation-states, and through Israeli policy reports about how to fight BDS activism, such as one titled "The 'Soft Warfare' against Israel."[11] But as Bill Mullen points out in an astute analysis of the war over BDS: "The battle between BDS and the Israeli Occupation is an asymmetrical one. On one side is Israel with one of the largest militaries in the world, capitalized by the EU and Gulf States, a trade partner to all of the major capitalist countries in the world, and still earning three million dollars a day in United States aid! That money and state power buy a tremendous amount of 'hard' and 'soft' power around the world." Clearly, this is an asymmetrical war, and a global one, as the BDS movement is indirectly challenging not just Israel's hegemony and its neoliberal imperial policies but also the alliances it has forged with erstwhile supporters of Palestine in the global South. The strategic partnerships that postcolonial states, such as Egypt and India, have forged with Israel have helped normalize it in the new world order since the decline of the Soviet Union and the ascendancy of the United States. As some say, in this moment the route to Washington is through Tel Aviv. Furthermore, as Ali Abunimah points out, Zionist organizations that oppose the BDS movement view "the war on critics of Israel as a war on the left more broadly."[12] The lines of this battle are thus important to clarify given that BDS is a progressive, social justice movement.

Mullen observes that supporters engaged in Palestine solidarity activism and BDS campaigns are fighting against a much more powerful enemy that flouts international human rights law and that also resorts to legal offensives:

> On our side is an ever-growing nonviolent social movement based in international law. We are effectively fighting a political guerilla war against a much bigger, more powerful opposition, with tactics and principles, many based in international law, which the other side doesn't have any interest in respecting. For example, Obama and the U.S. state have included anti-BDS language in the TPP (Transpacific Trade Agreement), and Governor Cuomo in New York has by executive order threatened to strip state funding from people or entities who are involved in BDS work—even though boycott is protected under the Constitution! The challenge we face is to fight simultaneously on these fronts—lawfare, uneven capitalization, against Israeli militarization and violence—while growing the movement.

As Mullen points out, the invocation of human rights and legal justice, which are core to the BDS principles, can seem futile if the antiboycott movement, and Israel, simply does not care about the law and adhering to rights. But this is precisely the conundrum that critical theorists have described as the "state of exception" in modern imperial states that exercise domination and inflict racial violence in defiance of, or sometimes through, the law and rights.[13] The BDS movement is an interesting case study in this regard, for it helps expose the paradox of rightlessness for Palestinians as well as the complicity of liberal democratic states in enforcing this deprivation of rights, as I will discuss in Chapter 4.

But the immense "hard" and "soft power" that Israel and its defenders have wielded against the boycott and BDS movement, as Mullen observes, is also precisely an index of the movement's strength. Extending his metaphor of guerilla warfare, the global, grassroots, and relatively underfunded BDS movement has managed to pose a real threat to the Goliath that is the U.S.-Israel alliance. Israel cannot afford to be seen as a "rogue state" condemned by the international community and lose its exceptional impunity. Israel cares deeply about its global image; it is invested in maintaining the mythology of being a modern western state in a sea of "barbaric" Arab nations, a state that must constantly go to war and maintain its military occupation to protect itself. According to Netanyahu, it is "the most embattled democracy on earth."[14] Not to overwork the metaphor, but the small slingshot represented by BDS throws stones at Israel where it hurts, rupturing the self-produced image of a liberal democratic state that has the right to assert its own hegemony as it pleases, internally and externally. This is also why the academic (and cultural) boycott is an effective, and appropriate, political weapon to use in the case of Israel.[15]

THE BACKLASH NETWORK

The attack has put the BDS movement on the defensive, so even if the assaults on the boycott campaign violate legal rights to freedom of expression, they can consume a great deal of energy for activists. Boycott advocates have to confront backlash by a global network that includes Israeli as well as U.S.-based organizations, elites, and political activists. Abunimah has uncovered and documented the strategies used by right-wing as well as liberal Zionist groups to combat the BDS movement, showing how organizations such as the Israeli legal advocacy group Shurat HaDin are involved in aggressive campaigns and legal threats targeting U.S. academics who support BDS (for example, USACBI organizer David Klein at California State University–Northridge), and work in tandem with Israeli intelligence agencies, thus acting as a "civilian front for the Israeli government."[16] As David Palumbo-Liu notes: "Paradoxically, because we are winning, we are being taken much more seriously. The hard right turn in Israeli politics, which is driving Netanyahu even further right, has brought with it more stringent and more well-funded campaigns to kill BDS. The collusion between Israeli state organs and U.S.-based organizations, funded by Sheldon Adelson and the Koch brothers and others, and supported by people like Hillary Clinton, has come out in force."

In March 2015, the International Jewish Anti-Zionist Network (IJAN) published a remarkable report based on detailed research about the "Zionist backlash network." It discovered that about a dozen extremely wealthy individuals have funded this network and channeled their money through intermediary organizations, such as donor-advised funds and community foundations and interest groups—for example, Daniel Pipes's Middle East Forum.[17] The organizations that are part of the network overlap and collaborate with one another, and are funded by powerful right-wing donors who support pro-Israel propaganda and anti-Arab and anti-Muslim policies as well as profit from Israel's policies and wars in the Middle East, since they also invest in the weapons and energy industries.

As noted by Palumbo-Liu, Adelson and the Koch brothers are part of this right-wing Zionist backlash network, as are the Koret, Becker, and Scaife Foundations. The network also funds attacks on queer movements, labor organizations, public education, and social welfare programs in general, according to the IJAN report. These donors have helped create a network of think tanks and media outlets that like the Reut Institute are key to orchestrating the Zionist backlash and framing BDS as an "existential threat" to Israel, a dramatic and entirely unfounded message that is then reproduced by Zionist activists and disseminated in the U.S. mainstream media without critical interrogation. The IJAN report notes some of the organizations that are part of this backlash network: the Anti-Defamation League (ADL), AMCHA Initiative, Brandeis Center, Simon Wiesenthal Center, the David Project, Israel on Campus Coalition, Stand with Us, and the Zionist Organization of America.[18] It is striking that all of the organizations on this list have targeted academics and universities and undermined academic freedom vis-à-vis Palestine-Israel, often in concert with the Israeli consulate. They have paid students to disseminate *hasbara* on social media and funded counter-organizing campaigns on campuses, such as "Israel Peace Week," in response to "Israel Apartheid Week."[19]

Intense national campaigns specifically targeting the academic boycott have been orchestrated and funded by Zionist organizations, such as the ADL, American Israel Public Affairs Committee (AIPAC), the Israel on Campus Coalition, AMCHA, and the Zionist Organization of America, and there have been blacklists of pro-BDS academics and students by the David Horowitz Freedom Center and murky groups such as Canary Mission. As Rajini Srikanth notes, these campaigns have escalated to the level of state and federal legislation, using the strategy of right-wing "lawfare":

> The Canary Mission and the David Horowitz Freedom Center are targeting BDS and academic boycott supporters and mounting a vicious campaign of vilification against students and faculty by labeling them "Jew haters" and "terrorists".... The political landscape is marked by the adoption of anti-BDS legislation in several states (Georgia, Florida, Illinois, South Carolina, Indiana, and Arizona), and efforts are underway in other states as well as in the U.S. Congress to make BDS activities illegal.... The most significant challenges to the boycott movement currently are the anti-BDS legislation in various states and the increased efforts by Zionist groups to target students, faculty, and other members of the academy.... The tactic of both these campaigns is to intensify intimidation and create a climate of fear.

The Zionist organizations discussed in the IJAN report have been involved in sponsoring the anti-BDS legislation mentioned by Srikanth. Zionist groups have also relied on tactics of intimidation, harassment, and defamation to create a chilling climate that Omar Barghouti and others have described as a "new McCarthyism."[20] Blacklists have long been used to intimidate academics and students who support the boycott or are engaged in BDS activism, continuing a tradition begun by Zionist activist Daniel Pipes's Campus Watch and adopted by Horowitz, as Srikanth points out, as well as newer groups such as AMCHA and Canary Mission. The ADL has a long history of blacklisting and harassment of faculty who are critical of Israel, such as Noam Chomsky and William Robinson, a sociologist at UC Santa Barbara, who was accused of anti-Semitism for his critique of Israel's war on Gaza in 2009.[21]

Blacklisting singles out individuals in order to send a message that others will be similarly targeted; that is, it stokes a politics of fear. Canary Mission has even threatened on its website that it will send the names of students to prospective employers, so it represents a personal as well as economic threat. Cynthia Franklin (who has been blacklisted by Canary Mission herself) observes "the chilling effect that well-funded Zionist organizations such as the Horowitz Freedom Center or the Campus Maccabees have, along with the anonymous cyber-stalking, bullying, and harassment that groups such as Canary Mission engage in when they post photos and personal information about students and slander these students for being critical of Israel, often directing tweets to students' universities and employers at an hourly rate." These tactics of fearmongering dissuade many who are more fainthearted, anxious, or economically insecure from BDS activism, especially students and untenured and contingent faculty but also tenured faculty who worry about reprisals and negative publicity.

Blacklists are selective in nature and rely on cherry-picking, but it is this very arbitrariness that makes people afraid and inclined to censor themselves, thus contributing to self-surveillance and self-policing and undermining academic freedom. For example, Horowitz published a highly inflammatory ad in the *New York Times* in 2012 attacking the boycott (and likening it to the Holocaust), which included a rather random assortment of boycott supporters among graduate students and faculty from across the United States.[22] Yet ironically, the AMCHA blacklist that has mapped campuses where there is strong BDS support (described as an "Anti-Semitism Tracker"), and other lists, have also helped compile useful data for the boycott movement.[23] Many scholar-activists have tried to counter the chilling effect of blacklists by reframing their inclusion as a badge of honor or by signing up themselves, attempting to subvert a tactic designed to produce shame and fear (as in the case of faculty who signed up to be included in the right-wing Professor Watch blacklist after Trump's election).

The backlash network has had a significant impact on student activism and the growing BDS movement on campuses. For instance, in 2010, the ADL blacklisted Students for Justice in Palestine (SJP) as one of the top-ten anti-Israel organizations in the United States—along with the Muslim Student Association, the leftist antiwar coalition ANSWER, and Jewish Voice for Peace—for daring to "accuse Israel of racism, oppression and human rights violations."[24] As SJP activists began using creative protest strategies—erecting mock checkpoints and simulacra of the Israeli "security wall" in the middle of campuses—the racial politics of Israeli state technologies of policing, segregation, encampment, collective punishment, and displacement of Arabs and Muslims erupted into plain sight in the U.S. academy. These protests provoked a vicious backlash from those who had long sought to suppress these "facts on the ground" and support the Israeli state's exceptionalism, including in the academy. The ADL has long masqueraded as an antiracist organization advocating for civil rights—except in the case of Palestine-Israel, where it *supports* racial discrimination and the suspension of civil rights.[25] As Steven Salaita argues, groups such as the ADL have used the language of liberal humanism and tolerance, civil rights, and antiracism to promote and consolidate the common sense that "support for Israel is a prerequisite of responsible multicultural citizenship," which is nowhere more evident than in the U.S. academy.[26] Salaita incisively observes that this contradiction arises from a situation in which "support for Israel is actually necessitous of proper multicultural consciousness" for academics and is thus considered normative and apolitical, while support for Palestinian rights is considered indecently "political."[27] The academic battle over the permissibility and boundaries of knowledge production about Palestine-Israel has thus become one of the most charged sites in the academic culture wars. Student activists and divestment organizers and supporters have been at the center of these battles on campus, as well as academics who are involved in BDS and Palestine solidarity activism or are simply daring to be critical of Israel in their classroom teaching, writing, and research.

THE CULTURAL AND RACIAL WARS

The forces arrayed against the academic boycott and BDS movement also oppose many social justice and progressive movements in the United States, not just Palestine solidarity activism. At the same time, the politics of the boycott is often contradictory given the alignment of liberal, not just right-wing, Zionist activists against BDS, sometimes through an obfuscating argument about the role of academic freedom. Abunimah's analysis of the multipronged campaign by Zionist activists and organizations targeting scholars underscores that "these attacks were also used as levers for a much broader assault on the independence of universities by individuals and organizations intent on curtailing dissent or critical inquiry related to U.S. global power and hegemony."[28] The boycott and BDS are a threat not just to the Israel lobby and Zionist state forces but also to U.S. imperial hegemony, which relies on Israel as a special ally in a strategic region, and to right-wing U.S. forces that uphold this hegemony. The enduring U.S.-Israel relationship has been shored up by a cultural discourse delegitimizing Palestinian rights to freedom (including academic freedom) that is Islamophobic as well as Arabophobic and is imbricated with racist, elitist, and homophobic right-wing movements.[29] Franklin notes: "In the U.S., one of the noteworthy impacts of BDS has been to create space to analyze and also to organize against not only the imperial violence and racism that structures the Israeli state, but also to understand how Zionism articulates with a host of other ills that must simultaneously be opposed. I am thinking here of the class-, gendered-, and race-based repression and violence that comes with neoliberalism, corporatization of the academy, White supremacy, Islamophobia, the prison-industrial-complex, heteropatriarchy, the list goes on."

In other words, the boycott and BDS are embedded in the larger culture wars in the United States as the right pushes back against progressive struggles and given that the Palestine question is entangled with the post–9/11 debates over Islam, immigration, race, gender, sexuality, and nationalism.

For example, the counter-campaign waged against the ASA after it adopted the resolution in 2013 in many cases rested on arguments based not just on academic freedom but on racism, intellectual conservatism, and the academic privilege of White U.S. scholars. The vitriolic letters and editorials that poured forth by opponents of the academic boycott rested on the argument that the boycott was anti-Semitic, without any mention of the anti-Palestinian racism upheld by U.S. support for Israel. Some critics of the boycott denounced the ASA for not being respectful of past (White) presidents of the ASA who opposed the resolution, charging that it emerged only from a "small but vocal minority" within the association and lamenting the intellectual currents that had corrupted the hallowed field as a stable, nonthreatening national institution. Other statements were more overtly racist, elitist, and homophobic in their attempt to silence and intimidate ASA members and supporters, given that the association had increasingly become a space for radical scholar activists, notably academics of color or those working in critical race studies and queer studies (including those in the ASA leadership who endorsed the resolution, especially then-president Curtis Marez and incoming president Lisa Duggan). This is not surprising given that Zionism is a racist, colonialist ideology, but the campaign by Zionist sympathizers made clear that this was a cultural and racial battle.

Palumbo-Liu notes the deepening cross-racial solidarity forged through BDS and the boycott movement that is so threatening to opponents of BDS: "Movement for Black Lives' endorsement of BDS, in a very vocal and system way, is huge, but also other minority groups and religious groups, including Clinton's own church, have come through with divestment measures, and when union dockworkers refuse to unload Israeli freighters, that is an amazing testament." One of the important resources the BDS movement has in its arsenal is indeed the growing "lines of solidarity" with other movements for social justice in the United States and increasing interracial coalition building, which is extremely threatening to Zionists. For example, in 2012, the major Chicanx student organization, MEChA (Movimiento Estudiantil Chican@ de Aztlan), officially endorsed BDS, and in a powerful statement of anticolonial and antiracist solidarity, MEChA activists declared, "Our Raza can relate to the concept of invasion, dispossession, occupation, exploitation, and discrimination."[30] In 2015, over one thousand Black scholars, artists, students, and organizations signed a statement of solidarity with Palestine—including Angela Davis, Cornel West, and Talib Kweli.[31] In the same year, a video featuring several artists of color supporting the growing cultural boycott of Israel (supported or honored by Alice Walker, Lauryn Hill, Talib Kweli, Santana, Stevie Wonder, and Mira Nair, among many other artists refusing to perform in Israel) was released by Adalah-New York, with the powerful proclamation: "How can I tour in Israel knowing that Palestinian artists are denied the right to travel?"[32] Growing out of the vigorous Black Lives Matter movement and the transnational solidarity forged through campaigns such as Ferguson 2 Gaza against police violence in, and collaboration between, Israel and the United States, a collective of over fifty Black organizations constituting the Movement for Black Lives (M4BL) issued a political statement in 2016, in which they publicly supported BDS.[33]

Cynthia Franklin, who is herself involved in the Hawai'i Coalition for Justice in Palestine (HCJP) and University of Hawai'i Students and Faculty for Justice in Palestine, reflects on the cross-movement solidarity forged through BDS:

> To draw on Darnell Moore and Sa'ed Atshan's formulation, the "reciprocal solidarities" that have been emerging as those in BDS and other social justice movements come together is resulting not only in emotionally sustaining shared stories and forms of community, but also in concrete forms of mobilization and calls to action for struggles that are at once articulated and place based. The historic M4BL Platform, and its support for BDS, is one example of this; another is Palestinian support for Native Peoples in North America organizing against the Dakota Pipeline. This is the result of organizers in different movements learning from and supporting each other in struggles that are at once articulated and sometimes distinct.

Israeli and Zionist think tanks, such as the Reut Institute, have explicitly declared that they are very concerned about the spread of Palestine solidarity activism among African Americans, Asian Americans, Chicanx, and Native Americans. Zionist groups have actively tried to recruit people of color and queers to defend Israel, engaging in strategies of what could be called blackwashing, brownwashing, or pinkwashing. The war of legitimacy waged by Israel is fought in an era of multicultural politics and in a moment when questions of race, gender, and sexuality are increasingly paramount. The strategy to relegitimize Israel by painting it as a nation that is gay-friendly, and thus modern, western, and democratic, has been critiqued by queer studies scholars, such as Jasbir Puar, and Palestinian queer activists as a form of "pinkwashing" settler colonialism and apartheid.[34] Zionist organizations have also tried to recruit African Americans and students of color to go on funded trips to Israel and work for the Israel lobby in Washington, DC, through programs such as the African American pro-Israel lobby organization, the Vanguard Leadership Group.[35] Vanguard, which has recruited student leaders from historically Black colleges and is funded by AIPAC and other programs targeting people of color to become alibis for Israel, represents a form of blackwashing or brownwashing in this war of legitimacy.[36] Similarly, a "redwashing" campaign has solicited Native Americans as spokespersons publicly critical of BDS;[37] this is perhaps one of the most acutely paradoxical (and disturbing) forms of backlash given that it attempts to pit one indigenous group struggling for survival in a settler state against another.[38] In doing so, it also engages in a denial of settler coloniality in both North America and Palestine.

These forms of pinkwashing, black- and brownwashing, redwashing, or greenwashing (that is, painting Israel as environmentally friendly, despite its devastation of the environment), or even what Curtis Marez calls "STEMwashing" or "knowledge washing" (portraying Israel as a uniquely technologically innovative "start-up nation"), are all strategies developed by defenders of Israel to suppress the growing solidarity with Palestine that has permeated many different movements for social justice. These strategies target liberals and progressives and increasingly people of color, thus shedding light on the cultural and racial wars that rage over the implications of the boycott and BDS for our contemporary political moment. As Palestinian scholar, activist, and USACBI cofounder Nada Elia reflects: "The boycott movement is growing in leaps and bounds as BDS activists grasp the connectedness of our own struggle with that of other disenfranchised communities. This coming together, around manifestations of the same oppressive systems (racism, criminalization of entire communities deemed "undesirable" and expendable by the ruling elite, etc.) is one of the more positive developments in recent activism, proving that, together, we are greater than the sum of our parts."

The boycott is also central to the cultural and racial wars over the meaning of Zionism, both in its right-wing and liberal variants. It is important to note the ways the backlash against the boycott has also emanated from liberal quarters, or from academics presumed to be progressive if not leftist. For instance, the politics of the American Association for University Professors (AAUP) and its past president, Cary Nelson (who works with the Israel on Campus Coalition), in relation to Palestine and Zionism, were exposed in their public denunciations of the boycott and concerted pressure on the ASA to uphold the dominant, institutionalized definition of academic freedom, which precludes the right to education and freedom of Palestinians, as discussed in Chapter 2. Nelson's Zionist politics (professed in his book *No University Is an Island*) became even more apparent in his attacks on Salaita after the latter's firing in 2014 by the University of Illinois at Urbana-Champaign (where Nelson teaches).[39] David

Lloyd and Malini Schuller, in an essay originally published in a special issue of the (AAUP's own) *Journal of Academic Freedom,* point out that while the AAUP supported divestment from South Africa, "the academic freedom extolled by the AAUP is a geopolitically based privilege rather than a historical right," for the AAUP's opposition to the "academic and cultural boycott of Israeli universities effectively promoted the idea of Israel as a state of exception."[40] Lloyd and Schuller describe this presumably liberal politics of academic freedom as operating "under the aegis of a liberal humanism that ignores or even denies colonialism or racial oppression." It is also important to describe it as an expression of liberal anti-Arab racism.[41]

Critics of BDS such as Nelson represent a cultural front of Zionism that includes a desire to defend Israel and protect its putatively democratic nature, invoking the notion of "saving Israel's soul," as Salaita himself analyzed in his excellent book *Israel's Dead Soul.*[42] These liberal Zionists are often critical of the occupation in the West Bank, but they are ultimately more concerned with the preservation of the Jewish state and its international legitimacy and criticize the state's policies inasmuch as they erode support for Israel and fuel the BDS movement. In some cases, liberal Zionists have even advocated for a limited BDS campaign, which may seem paradoxical, but their goal is to rein in Israel's excesses without challenging its founding logics. For example, Peter Beinart wrote a much-discussed op-ed in the *New York Times* in 2012, in which he called for a "Zionist BDS" movement based on a boycott of products from the illegal, Jewish-only settlements in the West Bank.[43] For self-proclaimed Zionist BDS advocates such as Beinart, calls for boycott and divestment of products from inside the Green Line (or Israel's borders) are tantamount to calls to end Israel's existence, while a settlement boycott upholds Zionism in "democratic Israel," legitimizing Zionism as a democratic nationalist project and protecting it from criticism of its racially discriminatory policies.

In a similar vein, after Israel's ban on entry of BDS activists in 2017 (passed a few weeks after Trump's anti-Muslim travel ban that targeted nationals of Arab and African states), a letter condemning it was signed by over one hundred Jewish studies scholars, nearly all Jewish American, who threatened to boycott Israel if the law was not rescinded; this included many who oppose BDS, and who argued that the law was turning Israel into an undemocratic state, thus shoring up support for BDS.[44] These claims fundamentally deny that a state built on racially distributed rights and Jewish-only privileges of citizenship is already undemocratic, and so exemplify the liberal Zionist attempt to counter BDS. Calls for a "Zionist BDS" aim to demarcate and delimit the scope of the burgeoning BDS movement and endorse some forms of boycott as permissible (from a particular Zionist standpoint) while rejecting others, especially the academic boycott, in order to curtail campaigns that denounce Israel's racism against Palestinian citizens or describe it as an apartheid or colonial state. Yet in 2015, two Jewish academics from Harvard University and the University of Chicago, who were self-declared "lifelong Zionists," acknowledged that apartheid was creeping into Israel, that its denial of "basic rights" to Palestinians was leading to its "international pariah status," and that the increasingly permanent nature of the occupation was threatening Israel's very existence; they called for a full boycott of Israeli products—but stopped short of an academic boycott.[45] Crucially, they failed to acknowledge that a Zionist state founded on a system of racial privilege, and only for its Jewish citizens, cannot be a democratic state, so their statement was ultimately also a call for Zionist BDS that could save Israel without disavowing the racial contradictions of a "Jewish-first democracy."

THE BOYCOTT AND JEWISH IDENTITY: ANTI-SEMITISM AND ANTI-ZIONISM

The Palestine solidarity movement and the boycott are also important staging grounds for a debate over the definition of anti-Semitism and the battle over Jewish identity and its allegiance to Israel and Zionism. One of the key tactics of the Zionist backlash network, as documented by IJAN's report, is to "make false claims of anti-Semitism" based on the premise that Israel and Zionism are identical to Judaism and all Jews, so that criticism of Israel and Zionism is automatically anti-Semitic. Zionist activists, such as the founder of the Reut Institute, have consistently described BDS as representing "a new form of anti-Semitism."[46] Some antiboycott campaigns have resorted to smear campaigns that are highly personalized, very public attacks vilifying individuals as anti-Semitic and racist, including defamatory allegations about personal behavior. Horowitz's backlash campaign includes the use of posters plastered on campuses across the United States with images and names of academics (such as Angela Davis, Robin Kelley, David Theo Goldberg, and Rabab Abdulhadi) and students involved with BDS, SJP, or Muslim Student Association (MSA) activism; the posters are emblazoned with accusations of anti-Semitism, "Jew hatred," and support of terrorism, as well as labeling BDS a "Hamas-inspired genocidal campaign" against the Jewish state.[47] The red herring of "anti-Semitism" has long been a central plank in the attack on Palestine solidarity activism, and it functions as a substitute for a political counterargument, or indeed a moral one, given that this allegation is highly charged and sensitive in the United States, as in Europe.

The charge that the academic boycott of Israel is anti-Semitic was leveled against the ASA boycott resolution and every single boycott resolution and BDS campaign before and since. Yet as IJAN activists have pointed out, and as Alex Lubin also notes, it is important "to disaggregate Jewish identity from Israeli state policy. The boycott call is not a boycott of Jews, or of any individuals, but of institutions that are complicit in the occupation."[48] This latter point is extremely important given that opponents of the academic boycott have routinely obfuscated the fact that PACBI's call for boycott targets Israeli academic institutions, *not individuals*, based on an ethical principle against blacklisting academics, yet the boycott has been tarred with false allegations of singling out Israeli and Jewish academics. This has been in many cases an effective diversion from the very real personalized attacks on scholars and students who do support the boycott or are critical of Israel—including racist attacks on and smear campaigns against Palestinian, Arab, and Muslim academics as well as Jewish advocates of the boycott. The anti-BDS backlash thus deepens a climate of academic precarity and insecurity and fortifies Islamophobia and anti-Arab racism.

Anti-Zionist Jewish Americans or those critical of Israel are often labeled "traitors" or "self-hating" Jews. Lubin observes that among Jewish American critics of Israel, too, are those who are critical of BDS or particularly resistant to supporting the boycott, and at the root of these anxieties is often an emotional and deeply held attachment to Israel intertwined with the history of the Holocaust and family narratives of survival and collective identity. Yet as Hedy Epstein, Lillian Rosegarten,

Norman Finkelstein, and Jewish survivors of the Holocaust have argued, experiences of anti-Semitic violence (in Europe) cannot be used as a rationale for racist violence against or erasure of another people's national identity (in Palestine). One could argue that the assumption that all Jewish people have an inherent, identical view when it comes to Israel and Zionism is in itself anti-Semitic because it brands an entire people, based on their religion, and assumes their automatic and unthinking support for Israel. Furthermore, framing the boycott as anti-Semitic and an "existential" threat to Israel, and to the Jewish people collectively (as conflated by Zionists), is dangerous because it removes the boycott from an intellectual and political discussion, based on facts on the ground and historical realities, to a purely emotional, and often highly distorted, narrative.

The BDS movement and the boycott have been attacked as expressions of a new form of anti-Semitism by the ADL and other Zionist groups that regularly intervene in college campuses and report cases of anti-Semitism to university administrations, using a definition that conflates it with "anti-Israelism" and thus promotes the indivisibility of Israel and Jewishness.[49] This tactic has been taken to new levels in legal campaigns to define campus activism critical of Israel as anti-Semitic, hence racist, and hence in violation of Title VI of the Civil Rights Act.[50] The Israel lobby has utilized civil rights in its "lawfare" against Palestine solidarity activists and MSA and SJP chapters, having successfully lobbied the Department of Education's Office of Civil Rights to define anti-Semitism as a violation of Title VI protections.[51] The 1964 Civil Rights Act can potentially now be used to deem illegal criticisms of Israel as expressions of the "new anti-Semitism" on college campuses, and to deny federal funding to universities.[52] Abunimah notes the painful irony

that the "Civil Rights Act, borne out of the struggle to end institutionalized racism" can now "perversely, be used as another
weapon in the hands of anti-Palestinian bigots and would-be
censors aiming to silence dissent against Israel's institutionalized racism against Palestinians."[53] This is yet another instance
of right-wing (as well as liberal) Zionists strategically using the
language of antiracism to silence critiques of racism or racialized state policies. A California state assembly resolution, HR
35, passed in 2012 under pressure from Zionist groups, targeted
pro-Palestine activism and events, including BDS campaigns,
on campuses as anti-Semitic, exacerbating fear, repression, and
self-censorship among students and faculty in the region.[54]

Zionist organizations have increasingly also used the language of "anti-Israelism," a new term coined to replace the alibi
of alleged "anti-Semitism," as they realized that many supporters of Palestinian rights, including Jewish American activists,
were challenging this tactic; groups such as the David Project
have defined "anti-Israelism" as a form of "bigotry" and "hate
speech" rife on college campuses to be combated by "criminal
and civil legal proceedings," as well as by tactical resorts to
the language of tolerance, peace, dialogue, and coexistence.[55]
Aggressive lawfare and academic discipline is thus used in
tandem with the Trojan horse of multicultural civility discourse
for stifling and censuring criticism of Israel.

In 2015, Palestine Legal and the Center for Constitutional
Rights issued the first report to document the suppression of Palestine advocacy in the United States, titled "The Palestine Exception to the First Amendment," a homage to Salaita's pronounce-
ment about his case.[56] The report noted that the overwhelming
majority of cases of censorship, punishment, intrusive investigation, administrative sanctions, and criminal prosecution reported

by Palestinian rights advocates (while many are never reported) are from students and scholars.[57] The fear that Muslim, Arab, and Palestinian American students have about involvement with Palestinian rights activism due to the backlash and the worry that it will affect their educational and work opportunities, as a result of this lawfare and defamation, was also documented in a report to University of California president Mark Yudof in 2012 by a cluster of civil rights organizations (including the Center for Constitutional Rights, the Asian Law Caucus of San Francisco, and the Council on American-Islamic Relations).[58] That said, the Department of Education's Office of Civil Rights threw out the Title VI complaints filed against three UC campuses since 2011, for allegedly enabling a climate of anti-Semitism due to Palestine solidarity protests, as having no legal basis.[59] The American Civil Liberties Union and Center for Constitutional Rights condemned the lawsuits as targeting student activism and political speech protected by the First Amendment, in effect creating a chilling campus climate for groups such as SJP and MSA; the Palestine Legal report did the same.[60] This challenges the claims that the BDS movement and criticism of Israel make Jewish students feel "unsafe" or create a hostile learning environment, which has provided the basis for allegations against well-known Palestinian scholars as well as attempts to counter student divestment campaigns. There is a crisis of academic freedom on U.S. campuses and a climate of fear and hostility experienced by BDS supporters targeted by blacklisting, threats, and intimidation coordinated by the anti-BDS network.

At the same time, the Zionist anti-BDS narrative pivoting on charges of anti-Semitism and a presumption of an inherent Jewish allegiance to Israel is increasingly challenged by vocal and energetic Jewish American BDS advocates and anti-Zionists, including in the academy. A few of the Jewish American scholar-activists in the boycott movement whom I interviewed spoke of the personal break they made with allegiance to Zionism, a politics often adopted or imposed through family affiliations. For example, Lisa Rofel reflected:

> For some years prior to my involvement in the academic boycott movement, I had been rethinking my relationship as an American Jew, who had been raised as Orthodox, to the state of Israel. Step by step I had been shedding the ideologies I had been taught as a child and learning about the realities of the Israeli occupation. As I read more about the history of the formation of Israel and its ongoing colonial practices towards Palestinians, I came to realize that the whole "peace" process was a sham, geared toward allowing Israel to continue business as usual. I had long been a critic of U.S. imperialism, and it was clear that Israel could not continue as a settler colonial state without the vast amount of military aid it receives from the U.S.
>
> I feel that since the horrendous violence and dehumanization that the Israeli state perpetrates against Palestinians is done in my name, both as an American and as a Jew, I have a responsibility to speak out and do something to oppose this violence.

In a similar vein, Jordy Rosenberg recalled that their experience of living in Israel led to a rupture of these ideological affinities, embedded in family and cultural ties:

> Our family was deeply embedded in the Zionist project, although in that typically assimilated U.S. way which expressed discomfort with more overt forms of Israeli violence but an affection for and attachment to the state of Israel nonetheless. These contradictions came to a head, for me, in 1988, when I was sent to do support work for the Israeli army on a base outside Jerusalem during the first Intifada. As a teenager who considered themselves generally "anti-war," and who had participated regularly in antiapartheid and

antipolice brutality rallies in New York City, where I grew up, living on the army base clarified for me that it was not possible to hold
the positions that I did and make an exception for Israel.

... On arriving at the base, I understood immediately one simple
fact: the mammoth arsenal of military equipment that it was my job
to wash down (tanks), clean out (machine guns), and pack (duffel
bags full of artillery) was being deployed to displace and dispossess
an indigenous people. I refused to do this work on the reasoning
that [it] would contribute to violence against Palestinians.

Similarly, Franklin reflects on how she became disabused of
Zionist mythologies, ultimately disavowing her family's affec-
tive ties with Israel:

I grew up in a nonreligious Jewish, de facto Zionist home. I neither
shared nor questioned my paternal grandparents' love for Israel. It
was not until the mid-1980s that I became aware that the foundation
of Israel as a Jewish state depended upon the expulsion of hundreds
of thousands of Palestinians. Via work in life writing studies—on
Edward Said and through attention to the narratives of the ISM
[International Solidarity Movement] when coediting a journal
issue on testimony and witnessing—Palestine became a scholarly
interest.

Franklin also observes how her scholarly interest in Palestine
propelled her politicization after encountering Zionist blow-
back: "Through this work, I discovered that when it comes to
Palestine, only with the greatest of difficulty can research not
lead to political involvement. First, to even acknowledge Palestinians' existence or right to narrate propels one into politics: I
soon found myself charged with anti-Semitism and chastised for
behaving 'scandalously' because of a conference paper's subject
matter." The irony of accusing a (progressive-left) Jewish American of anti-Semitism in order to silence her and block research
is, of course, acute. This is perhaps the *real* scandal.

But it is also clear that personal experiences with Zionist backlash actually often catalyze greater political engagement and constitute a growing archive of politicization around BDS. David Palumbo-Liu, a leading Asian American studies scholar, shared a similar story of how he became galvanized to advocate for the academic boycott due to his encounter with Zionist attacks and media censorship. He recalled his experience following the AAAS boycott resolution in 2013:

> The discussion of the boycott at the Association for Asian American Studies was critical to my understanding of how the boycott touched on so many issues at once. This was made particularly clear when Jonathan Marks wrote a dismissive, insulting, and racist op-ed in *Inside Higher Education* regarding the AAAS vote. I could not let that stand, and in writing my rebuttal,[61] and arguing with the editors about getting my statement into print (and that series of e-mail exchanges grew more and more ludicrous each day), I learned a great deal about how getting even a small bit of criticism of Israel into the public eye was near impossible. That, along with the silencing of debate about Israel-Palestine, made me more active in the boycott movement.

Palumbo-Liu is known as a progressive public intellectual who writes about politics in several alternative media venues, and he reflected thoughtfully on what it meant to confront the taboo on criticizing Israel: "I went into university teaching because of the rich world of ideas and conversation it was supposed to offer. It astounded me that there was one single subject that could not be talked about without dire consequences. In sum—as a long-time student of comparative studies in race and ethnicity, and literary studies, I was drawn to the issue of Israel-Palestine, and the more I learned about it, the more I appreciated the care, intelligence, and passion for justice that informs the core of BDS."

Palumbo-Liu went on to become an active member of USAC-BI's organizing collective and has indeed become one of the most prolific and regular commentators in the progressive media on issues related to BDS, Palestine, and academic freedom, writing posts regularly for *Huffington Post* and *Salon*. So (Zionist) repression creates its own vigorous and popular resistance, by scholars and activists from a range of racial backgrounds and disciplinary locations, who bring their varied experiences of political involvement in progressive struggles to the boycott campaign

THE SMOKESCREEN
OF ACADEMIC FREEDOM

One of the key planks of the countermovement against the academic boycott is that it undermines academic freedom, namely, that it is an attack primarily on the academic freedom of supporters of Israel. In many cases, antiboycott critics charge that the boycott is an anti-Semitic attack on Jewish American and Jewish Israeli academic freedom because it will somehow silence pro-Israel voices and isolate Israeli scholars working at Israeli universities. Yet as noted above, the academic boycott targets only Israeli institutions (that are aligned with the state), and not individual Israeli scholars. This distorted argument and the disingenuous deployment of the language of academic freedom is part of a larger strategy by right-wing and neoconservative activists in the culture wars to use notions of "tolerance" and "diversity" to shut down left critiques. Indeed, right-wing Zionist groups such as Horowitz's Students for Academic Freedom have used the notion of "intellectual pluralism" to police teaching and invoked academic freedom as a new ideological battle cry for the right. The U.S. State Department opened the door for such appropriation of the language of antiracism and intolerance by adopting a very broad definition of anti-Semitism in 2010 that included the infamous "3 D's" in specifically addressing criticism of Israel: demonizing Israel, applying "double standards" to Israel, and delegitimizing Israel.[62] All of these could be usefully applied to tar the entire BDS movement with the brush of anti-Semitism and intolerance, and this has indeed been the case.

For example, in January 2016, after a long and controversial process entailing lobbying by Zionist organizations and protests by Palestinian rights and Jewish solidarity activists, the University of California Regents issued a report on the "Principles of Intolerance," which singled out anti-Semitism as *the* major problem of intolerance on UC campuses, claiming there was an increase in incidents of anti-Semitism on campuses (when in fact other organizations such as Jewish Voice for Peace point out that there has been a decrease) and condemning "anti-Semitism, anti-Semitic forms of anti-Zionism, and other forms of discrimination."[63] While anti-Semitism must be unequivocally denounced, anti-Zionism is hitched to anti-Semitism in this statement with no precise definition of what it means, paving the way again for blanket censorship of anti-Zionism.[64] Yet in one of the first instances, to my knowledge, of collective pushback on this issue by UC academics at large—including those not necessarily involved with the Palestine movement—the UC Academic Senate issued a letter criticizing the censure of anti-Zionism in the Regents' Principles on Intolerance and upholding the right of faculty to oppose, debate, and discuss Zionism.[65]

The boycott and BDS have of course been at the center of the most intense debates over academic freedom and the boundaries of "permissible" discussion of Israel in the U.S. academy, given the censorship of the boycott even among liberal and progressive scholars. There is no progressive politics per se built into the principle of academic freedom, and this is what makes it easily available for recuperation and resort by Zionists on the right as much as the left. One of the most striking cases of the dangerous use of academic freedom as a smokescreen for larger struggles over other kinds of freedoms is the case of censorship of BDS in the name of academic freedom. For instance, the AAUP's own conference on academic boycotts, slated to be held in 2006 in Bellagio, Italy, was canceled under pressure from Israeli and pro-Israel academics, presaging later controversies about the AAUP's stance on the boycott.[66] Lisa Taraki, a scholar at Bir Zeit University in the West Bank and PACBI founder, who was scheduled to present, incisively observed: "I think that the abstract ideas of academic freedom and the free exchange of ideas cannot be the only norms influencing the political engagement of academics. Often, when oppression characterizes all social and political relations and structures, as in the case of apartheid South Africa or indeed Palestine, there are equally important and sometimes more important freedoms that must be fought for, even—or I would say especially—by academics and intellectuals."[67] Omar Barghouti made a crucial point when he argued that the AAUP was "privileging academic freedom as above all other freedoms." He pointed out the racial fault lines at work: "Academic freedom, from this angle, becomes the exclusive privilege of some academics but not others."[68] Magid Shihade, a Palestinian academic at Bir Zeit and a founding member of USACBI, writes: "Boycotting Israeli institutions does not target individual Israeli academics. Academics in the United States can continue to collaborate with them. Furthermore, many progressive Israel academics have themselves called for boycott as the only alternative that can push for change. Finally, these arguments never take into consideration Palestinian academics and the harmful Israeli policies against them individually and against Palestinian academic institutions in general. Why do Palestinian academics matter less, if at all, in these debates?"[69]

As these Palestinian intellectuals and activists suggest, academic freedom cannot trump other rights to freedom (and other freedoms), namely, the right to freedom of mobility for students and scholars to attend college, to travel to conferences, to do research; the collective right to self-determination; the freedom from occupation and racial segregation; in essence, the freedom to live in peace, dignity, and equality. Shihade movingly documents in his essay about the boycott the many ways Palestinian students and scholars are denied the right to education and the daily struggles they must wage simply to study, attend school, gain university admission, do research, and teach as Palestinians; he reflects on his own long struggle and the racism, humiliation, and repression he encountered for years trying to gain access to education as a Palestinian growing up in Israel.[70] Shihade makes the powerful point: "In sum, there is *already a boycott against Palestinians* taking place both in Israel and in the United States."[71] Thus, these debates about the boycott, including among liberals and progressives, reveal a racial politics concerning *whose* freedom must be upheld, and a racialization of the human, for the freedoms of White scholars and academics in the global North are a greater cause of anxiety for many than those of scholars living under occupation and colonization on the other side of the "global color line" of human rights.[72]

The question of how the boycott does or does not shore up academic freedom thus illuminates the politics of race and colonialism, as it relates to Palestine, Zionism, human rights, and solidarity. Palestinian scholars who support the boycott highlight the selectivity of the principle of academic freedom—why South Africa and not Palestine?—and the ways in which the U.S. academy (like the Israeli academy) and professional associations such as the AAUP are firmly embedded in a political context, while pretending to be outside of it or above it.[73] Advocates of the academic boycott of Israeli institutions observe that it thus *supports* and enlarges academic freedom, including in the United States, and that it supports human rights for *all*—as was the case in the boycott of South African institutions.

CONCLUSION

The backlash against the boycott and BDS has underscored that the movement poses a real challenge to the material apparatus of Zionism and the ideological framework necessary to maintain Israel's policies of annihilation and racial violence over decades. In fact, an important antiracist challenge is waged in the work of the boycott movement and USACBI. It is this race politics that has made the boycott a challenging front on which to recruit U.S. scholars who have long had an uneasy and ambivalent relationship to the repressed race politics of settler colonialism in Palestine-Israel, many unwilling to denounce Zionism as racism even if this race politics and racial violence have been in plain view. The discourse of boycott helps challenge the inverted accusation of racism that is leveled against the BDS movement by revealing that it is Zionism and settler colonialism that are racist projects. It also interrupts a liberal multicultural framework of cross-cultural "dialogue" between Palestinians and Israelis, Jews and Muslims, and of interfaith tolerance as the solution to a religious conflict, which elides Zionism and anti-Palestinian racism.

This mobilization on behalf of Palestine solidarity activists, rather than being in a defensive mode, can continue to deepen knowledge production about Palestine-Israel and strengthen an antiracist, anticolonial politics. As Franklin observes, rather than "working in a reactive" mode, "In the face of attacks and obstacles, I do think it bears remembering that the ugliness of Zionist tactics exposes Zionism's deep structures, and that important educational work can happen in the process of organizing against these tactics." Echoing this view, Rofel comments, "In the U.S., the challenge is that we have to keep fighting off illegal—but well-funded—efforts to defeat the boycott movement while simultaneously trying to move forward." Several campaigns have been organized to defend academics and students facing backlash for Palestine solidarity and BDS activism and reprisals from university administrators; these have provided resources for support and created networks of solidarity. For example, Palestine Legal has published hard-hitting reports on what it calls the "Palestine exception to the First Amendment," providing information to activists about their political and academic rights; and the National Lawyers Guild has also compiled legal information for Palestine supporters and BDS activists.[74]

Many academic boycott organizers are on the frontlines of work to defend the movement, providing tools based on cumulative experience to support others facing backlash, while continuing to build the BDS movement.[75] For example, Nada Elia mentions that she is involved in "exposing the Canary Mission, and the Horowitz Center's blacklisting of faculty and students involved in activism for justice in Palestine, and organizing, locally, in the Seattle area, rapid response teams that respond to anti-BDS legislation." Organizing against lawfare and backlash has also brought together various BDS and Palestine solidarity organizations in coalitions that unite academics, lawyers, community activists, and students. Lastly, Rofel offers a note of wisdom about sustaining organizing in a difficult movement for the long haul: "Social movements take time to gather force and be effective. I want to encourage those who experience the hardships of this movement to remember we have a long-term goal."

The antiboycott backlash is increasingly resisted by coordinated and public efforts by academics, students, activist lawyers, and community activists, and has helped expose university administrators' complicity with repression and promotion of pro-Israel views. The archive of repression thus produces a counter-archive of testimonials of resistance, education, and rethinking—a dialectic that is immensely generative for the BDS movement. While the backlash is a source of genuine frustration and harm to many individuals, it is ultimately a club wielded by powerful forces against masses of ordinary people who keep rising up to challenge this hegemony that is in the service of racism, colonialism, and militarism. And in that sense, it is clear the backlash is, simply put, not working. In the following chapter, I will discuss the ways the boycott movement and BDS activism on campuses have fostered significant coalitions among social justice movements and reenergized academic activism. The boycott is at the center of battles over the neoliberal structuring of the university and academic labor, helping to advance a politics of decolonizing the academy.

FOUR

Academic Abolitionism

Boycott as Decolonization

This chapter explores how the boycott movement is on the front-lines of the struggle to democratize the neoliberal university, sparking solidarity among contingent academic workers, dissident and fugitive scholars, and activists. BDS is increasingly a part of campus campaigns challenging academic repression, austerity measures, surveillance, campus militarization, police brutality, the prison-industrial complex, and other apparatuses that constitute the new "normal" of U.S. higher education.[1] The boycott, I argue, is part of the larger struggle for academic abolitionism, or the movement to decolonize the university through radical transformation and resistance from within.[2] I briefly discuss the well-known case of Palestinian American scholar and boycott advocate Steven Salaita, which became part of a wider battle over faculty governance and autonomy and dramatically illustrated what is at stake in academic activism in support of the boycott. His case, and the solidarity movement it sparked, reveals what it means to fight for the right of U.S.-based scholars to support the boycott and challenge Zionism, while remembering that the object of the boycott is freedom for Palestinians from settler colonialism, and that these freedoms are indivisible. In this chapter, I draw on my interviews with Palestinian scholars and activists and discuss cross-movement organizing among academics to highlight how the academic boycott is part of a broader struggle for decolonization, here and in Palestine.

THE BOYCOTT AND ACADEMIC ACTIVISM

BDS campaigns in national academic associations and the work of USACBI have united faculty and graduate students across the United States and from various disciplines and fields, reenergizing a politics of internationalism and transnational solidarity. These campaigns have allowed academics to publicly and collectively reject collaboration with Israeli academic institutions and demand that U.S. academic institutions—so far mostly professional associations but also academic labor unions—take a principled stand in condemning Israel's occupation and wars and, in some cases, its colonial and racist policies too. This politics of refusal is part of larger efforts by scholars to transform the university into a site of struggle against militarization as well as racial and class oppression and to challenge U.S. imperial power and its proxies. The boycott, in particular, has been an important tool for winning political space and enlarging intellectual space, as I have explored in previous chapters.

However, another component of this academic struggle that has become increasingly visible is that of academic employment rights. In a context in which the university increasingly relies on part-time or contingent faculty for instruction, and full-time tenure track jobs are ever more scarce, there is a greater precarity of academic labor. Palestine is at the center of this condition of academic insecurity given the ongoing denial of employment, promotion, grant funding, and fellowships to scholars critical of Israel and engaged in BDS, and given the intimidation and censorship of academics advocating for boycott through defamation, harassment, and blacklisting, as discussed in Chapter 3. As a result of these witch hunts and academic embargoes, there is by now a class of scholars who have been stigmatized, demonized, and in some cases expelled from the academy, and who are often, literally, on the run, moving from one institution to the next or from one country to another—whom I would call fugitive scholars, building on Fred Moten and Stefano Harney's work on fugitive study.[3] Many of these scholars who end up in a liminal space of insecurity have dared to publicly criticize U.S. foreign policy and support for Israel and have lost their jobs or gone into academic exile, as in the cases of Salaita, Terri Ginsberg, Magid Shihade, Nada Elia, and many, many others. The experiences of these fugitive scholars painfully illustrate the policing of knowledge in the imperial university.[4]

The repression enacted through the policing of research, teaching, and speech related to Palestine-Israel is also part of the neoliberalization of the U.S. university, which in brief is a move toward privatization and an alignment of the university with corporate interests and away from its mission as a space for independent, critical thought and teaching. Powerful off-campus lobby groups and well-funded private organizations have colluded with university administrators in the restructuring of the academy, distorting and censoring research and pedagogy. The Palestine question is often the funnel of this neoliberal restructuring of the academy that involves corporatization as well as the erosion of the right to education as a public good, these being part of the greater shrinking of social welfare services in the neoliberal capitalist state and a deepening of social and economic inequality.[5]

Administrators in the neoliberal university are complicit with state interests in myriad ways and at different scales of collusion. For example, the California Scholars for Academic Freedom group issued a powerful statement in 2016,[6] denouncing the administration's cancelation of a course at UC Berkeley, "Palestine: A Settler Colonial Analysis," under pressure from over forty Zionist organizations. The statement went on to document a long list of similar cases of academic repression around the country, noting that this pattern has intensified over the past fifteen years and serves to protect the "interest of one foreign government, namely, Israel." The statement observes that "nothing presently compares to the problematic way that some university and college administrators have chosen to deal with this particular conflict, including advocating a censorious approach. Too often, university administrators concerned about donors have caved in to these outside pressures rather than make a robust defense of academic freedom."

The role of university administrators in this deformation of knowledge is significant, and academic repression happens in most instances with cooperation, *not* criticism, from those who have the power to defend academic freedom on behalf of faculty, students, and staff. In the case of critical pedagogy and campus activism related to Palestine-Israel, as discussed in the previous chapter, university administrators inevitably buckle under threats from alumni and donors. There is an element of cowardice or craven self-protection and economic self-interest here, as the university is increasingly remade in the image of a corporation, concerned about its image and "branding" in the educational marketplace, and its funding streams. Often there is also an element of ideological collusion between the university's managerial elites and Zionist interests when the former censor or clamp down on Palestine solidarity activism and student organizing; as Bill Mullen points out, "Most campuses refuse to stand up for these students, because their donors, their state-funding, their administrative leadership, their alumni often support Israel formally or informally."

The flip side of this academic repression is that Palestine is also at the center of challenges to the U.S. academic "establishment" and the neoliberalization of the university that makes academic labor so precarious. The case that most tragically illustrates how academic employment rights are eroded by the collusion of campus elites and Zionist interest groups is that of Palestinian American scholar and USACBI organizing collective member Steven Salaita. Salaita is a prolific American and comparative indigenous studies scholar whose many books have pioneered analyses at the intersections of Palestine studies, settler colonialism, Arab American identities and politics, and indigenous solidarities. In 2014, he was effectively fired from the University of Illinois–Urbana Champaign (UIUC) after being officially appointed as tenured professor in the Department of American Indian Studies. Salaita was a vocal BDS advocate and had published articles about the academic boycott as a supporter of the ASA resolution, which UIUC's administration publicly opposed along with a slew of other university chancellors who condemned the boycott vote in 2013.

Salaita was also active on social media, posting Tweets about a range of issues, including Israel's brutal war on Gaza in the summer of 2014, and he had long earned the ire of Zionist scholars and activists. In an unprecedented move, given that Salaita's appointment had been vetted by academic officials, Chancellor

Phyllis Wise sent a letter to Salaita in August 2014 terminating his job and justifying this in the name of preserving "civility" due to Zionist objections to Salaita's Tweets as being uncivil.[7] Yet having formally accepted the job offer, Salaita had already resigned his job at Virginia Tech and had even been assigned courses to teach at UIUC. This unprecedented cancellation of an employment offer created outrage among academics and others, which swelled into a national firestorm. While Salaita became the poster child for the crisis of academic freedom vis-à-vis Palestine, it was at great personal cost to him and his family, and the academic career of a brilliant scholar was wrecked.

UIUC's Committee on Academic Freedom and Tenure, and even the AAUP, denounced the university for its violation of academic rights and "academic due process," and academics and students at UIUC as well across the United States mobilized on his behalf.[8] A petition was circulated in solidarity with Salaita condemning the UIUC administration's decision and calling for his reinstatement; it garnered almost twenty thousand signatories.[9] Approximately five thousand academics signed a statement boycotting UIUC until Salaita's reinstatement, this being spearheaded by USACBI organizers in consultation with UIUC faculty; while others published articles and blog posts calling out the racism implicit in the discourse of "civility" and the upholding of Zionist interests by the university. Thus the campaign in solidarity with Salaita itself deployed the boycott as an instrument to protest a U.S. university's violation of academic freedom and academic employment rights.

The "Salaita affair" illuminated, once again, the ways that antiboycott and Zionist lobby groups interfere in and deform critical thought in the academy and erode employment rights.[10] Salaita's ejection from UIUC was in many ways the culmination of the backlash against the boycott movement documented in the previous chapter. It was also a test case for Zionist groups who had been ratcheting up their tactics of academic repression, as targeting a single, well-known individual sent a chilling message to others who might speak up as boldly and unapologetically as Salaita had done.

This was a vicious case of anti-Palestinian racism, targeting a pioneering and prolific Palestinian academic. It was also an erosion of the autonomy of American Indian studies, the department that had hired Salaita, and thus an instance of anti-indigenous repression, undermining indigenous scholars' self-determination in the arena of knowledge production. As Vicente Diaz, then a faculty member in American Indian studies at UIUC, observed: "I can only describe the university's actions as the intellectual negation of critical indigenous scholarship, and one that resonates with a longer history that is all-too-familiar to native peoples in particular: the will to eliminate the Native in the colonial interest of preserving the colonial occupation of the Native's land and in the interest of policing indigenous intellectual and especially indigenous political thought."[11] For Diaz and others, Salaita's firing was an attack on the vision of global indigenous solidarity that the American Indian studies department represented, and on the challenge to global settler colonialism that Salaita so powerfully expressed in his writing and his activism.[12] Salaita has reflected that his case exposed "the precariousness of American Indian and Indigenous studies in institutions motived by a pervasive and unnamed colonial logic, one that devalues AIS [American Indian studies] as a field and Native peoples as sovereign agents."[13]

The Salaita affair fueled collective mobilization on multiple fronts among academics and students, especially in American studies, ethnic and indigenous studies, and Palestine studies but also in other fields, given the shocking abrogation of academic freedom and employment rights it dramatized. Many academics who were not necessarily boycott supporters signed the petition on his behalf, given that they now wondered whether they would lose their teaching jobs, too, if they sent a Tweet that powerful interest groups did not like. Tithi Bhattacharya and Mullen revealed that Chancellor Wise and the UIUC board of trustees president served on the boards of corporations that do business in Israel and were also linked to prominent American Zionists affiliated with Israeli universities; subsequent investigations revealed that wealthy donors had secretly pressured the UIUC administration to fire Salaita.[14] The case underscored the collusion of Zionism and neoliberalism in the U.S. university. As documented by the International Jewish Anti-Zionist Network's (IJAN's) report *Business of Backlash,* discussed in the previous chapter, a network of Zionist organizations and funders holds powerful sway over university administrators in their management and disciplining of critical discussion of Palestine-Israel. But these assaults on the right to academic freedom and the right to teach have also provoked powerful movements of academic resistance and defense of academic labor rights, such as that in defense of Salaita, that include support for the boycott as one important plank.

These academic solidarity campaigns have foregrounded the importance of academic labor organizing and its connection to BDS and Zionist interventions in the academy. Bhattacharya and Mullen make an eloquent case for why we should "de-Zionize" the academy and argue that "faculty unionization" and BDS organizing on campus "should go hand in hand."[15] This is an important insight into the struggle to take back the university from neoliberal, corporate, and militarized interests. Indeed,

BDS activists have increasingly been at the fore of academic unions and waged successful divestment campaigns across the United States. As Jordy Rosenberg notes: "One area of organizing that represents a major development in Palestine solidarity organizing are the recent BDS resolutions passed by Graduate Student-Worker Unions at the University of Wisconsin (TAA/AFT Local 3220, the oldest graduate student labor union in the country), NYU (UAW 2110), University of Massachusetts (UAW 2322), and the University of California (UAW 2865)." Rosenberg also points out that these BDS campaigns have reinvigorated academic labor activism and also helped push back against mainstream union politics:

> Not only do several of these resolutions explicitly call for both divestment and academic boycott (Wisconsin, NYU, and the UC), but they represent courageous departures from the union bureaucracy and signal a turning tide in terms of the reawakening of progressive forces within labor unions. The TAA/AFT resolution is also notable in having explicitly tied its resolution around Palestine to another TAA/AFT resolution about solidarity with the "nationwide movement in support of racial and economic justice."
>
> I think it is also worth noting that although the UAW national leadership attempted to autocratically "nullify" UAW 2865's democratic vote, recently the NLRB [National Labor Relations Board] confirmed the legality of union support for BDS.

In fact, the UAW Local 2865, which represents thirteen thousand graduate employees at the University of California, became the first mainstream union in the United States to endorse divestment, in 2014, followed by the first endorsement of BDS by a national labor union, the United Electrical, Radio, and Machine Workers.[16] Importantly, the overwhelming vote in support of the UAW 2865 divestment resolution was accompanied by an individual pledge to support the academic boycott, endorsed by 52 percent of the graduate student workers who voted.[17] These victories illustrate the growing grassroots mobilization at the conjuncture of academic labor and BDS activism.

While faculty unions in the United States have not yet adopted BDS resolutions, which have largely been endorsed at the level of national professional academic associations—unlike in the United Kingdom, where there have been academic boycott campaigns in faculty unions—there is a growing movement of Faculty for Justice in Palestine (FJP) chapters across the United States. In response to a call by USACBI after the ASA boycott campaign, these autonomous groups have mobilized faculty and graduate students, and in some cases university staff, to work in solidarity with students on BDS campaigns; to resist censorship of teaching and research related to Palestine-Israel; and to make linkages between Palestinian freedom and other struggles for social, racial, and economic justice. For example, the mission statement of FJP-Davis declares:

> As educators at UC Davis we stand against all forms of colonialism, racism, and apartheid in that they are not compatible with universal education or emancipation. We stand in solidarity, therefore, with Students for Justice in Palestine and with Palestinians resisting occupation, warfare, displacement, and dispossession. We recognize further that their struggle is also one against the political and economic restructurings associated with global capital, and that principled opposition to one will also be principled opposition to the other.
>
> The Palestinian question has become the fulcrum of these struggles on university campuses, and students and faculty who are part of the Palestine solidarity movement are increasingly subject to surveillance, and criminalization. Thus, we view the movement for justice in Palestine as a crucial terrain for highlighting the defense of freedom of expression and political commitment within

the academy; the preservation of free inquiry, engaged pedagogy, and open scholarship; and the survival of egalitarian campus governance in the face of attacks by off-campus groups allied with unconditional United States support for the Israeli state.[18]

I cite this statement to illustrate the ways Palestine and BDS solidarity activism uniting faculty and graduate students are part of a broader, collective push for greater democratization of the university, and against the neoliberal Zionist interventions apparent in the Salaita case.

BDS AND ACADEMIC ABOLITIONISM

This united front to take back the space of the university from authoritarian repression, neoliberal corporatization, and Zionist influence will become even more evident in the Trump era, given that the vigorous faculty responses to Trump's election have followed and built on BDS organizing in recent years. The backlash against BDS advocates is now part of the growing attack on left movements and academics, including Black Lives Matter activists and Standing Rock Water Protectors protesting the Dakota Access Pipeline, both movements facing off against the U.S. state; this backlash has entailed antiprotest bills proposed by Republican legislators that are related to the wave of bills (often proposed by Democratic lawmakers, and passed by sixteen states thus far) silencing BDS and Palestinian rights activism. As an analyst from the Defending Dissent Foundation points out, "The bills aimed at silencing supporters for Palestinian human rights are anti-protest bills" that are part of the wider crackdown on social justice movements in the Trump era, but also earlier.[19] In other words, the BDS movement has emerged along with other recent progressive mass movements, and has been part of strengthened cross-movement alliances that were forged before Trump's election but continue to grow—for example, in current campus sanctuary activism across the United States in solidarity with undocumented immigrant communities and in protests against the anti-Muslim/Arab/African ban and plans to fortify the U.S.-Mexico border wall.

I consider this progressive-left academic solidarity forged in relation to the BDS movement along different axes of struggle to be a potential expression of academic abolitionism. The notion of academic abolitionism is not focused on redeeming the U.S. academy—just as it is ultimately not focused on redemption for the U.S. imperial state—as much as it is on going *beyond* the liberal discourse of academic freedom to highlight other kinds of freedoms, and un-freedoms. The boycott of Israeli academic institutions that are complicit with occupation and apartheid is only one component of a larger *politics of refusal* grounded in academic abolitionism. An abolitionist view challenges the complicity of the U.S. academy with global militarism, carceral regimes, and settler colonial circuits of power, in which Israel is a key player. Thus it suggests a radical structural transformation of the U.S. university that does not simply ask for *more* freedom for U.S. academics, such as to teach courses critical of Israel alongside other courses in the curriculum endorsing Israel, and on campuses where Israeli state funds are used for Brand Israel programs; this limited view of academic freedom based on a false notion of "balance" and diversity, and on individual employment rights, allows the material violence in Palestine to persist. Instead, left academic organizing and academic abolitionist visions emerging from BDS activism expose how the university is firmly embedded in the neoliberal, imperial settler state (and its proxies) and is a site of regulation of the political and economic order. This is based on "the popular and antiracist democratization of higher education" and the abolition of a society that builds prisons as a new form of slavery, that militarizes education, that inflicts lethal violence on racialized populations within and beyond its borders, that lets people suffer because they can't afford health care, that continues to degrade and erase indigenous lives.[20] Julia Oparah argues, for example, that scholars resisting the "militarization and prisonization of academia" must use their privilege to challenge the complicity of the academy with prison and military industries (and call for divestment) in order to work for the abolition of the academic-military-prison-industrial complex.[21]

Radical academic activism and boycott campaigns can also do the crucial work of highlighting links between settler universities in the United States and in Palestine, in tandem with growing scholarship that traces the links between settler colonialism in North America and Palestine-Israel. Settler colonialism takes different forms in Palestine-Israel and in the United States and has had different historical trajectories. In the context of the United States, the university is an institution that exists within a settler state; land-grant universities, specifically, are materially settler institutions, but all U.S. universities are located within a settler society and are thus settler universities. In this sense, they are a site in which the sovereignty and power of the settler state is upheld, directly and indirectly, and in which U.S. imperial policies are often legitimized, overtly or covertly, through expert knowledge production as well as through repression of resistant knowledges and policing of permissible discourse about settler coloniality.

Therefore, supporting the boycott and BDS movement also requires a commitment by U.S. scholars to decolonial politics and solidarity with indigenous people *here*. Salaita makes the important point that "BDS needs to be attentive to local politics wherever it is practiced," and "[in] North America, BDS should be more attuned to the wide-ranging and ongoing efforts to decolonize the continent."[22] Salaita has argued incisively in his book *Inter/nationalism: Decolonizing Native America and Palestine* that in positioning the boycott within the U.S. settler colonial landscape and in relationships of indigenous solidarity linking North America and Palestine, "BDS actually functions as an articulation of Native sovereignty, inside and beyond America."[23] He notes the importance for BDS advocates "to put Palestine into conversation with Native liberation struggles and make ourselves useful under their guidance and direction. Cultivating this focus is an ethical imperative because we are performing the work of decolonizing Palestine on ground that is itself colonized."[24] Salaita's notion of "inter/nationalism" provides scaffolding for the "commitment to mutual liberation" based on "decolonial thought and practice" that should be central to the BDS movement.[25] The academic boycott movement and the solidarity and struggle it engenders are thus also movements to decolonize the settler university, here and elsewhere.

THE BOYCOTT, ANTIRACISM, AND PALESTINIAN (UN)FREEDOM

The censorship and policing of the BDS movement and of faculty who support the boycott are deeply intertwined with the Zionist apparatus of repression in Palestine-Israel that violently suppresses any resistance to the displacement, dispossession, and annihilation of indigenous Palestinians. While the boycott's challenge to the lockdown on discussion of Palestine-Israel in the U.S. university is very significant, the focus of the academic boycott is ultimately, and crucially, the freedom and justice that are missing for our Palestinian colleagues and for the Palestinian people. In concluding this book, I want to turn to those whom the backlash has disappeared but whom the boycott movement aims to recenter, that is, Palestinian scholars and students, who are often absent figures in the U.S. academy, and their absent freedoms.

In the debate about the boycott there is a constant resort to the figure of the Israeli or the Jewish scholar, and her academic freedom and academic privilege, that displaces the figure of the Palestinian scholar. This is because Palestinians are ghosts in the U.S. academy. Not only are there few Palestinian scholars who manage to get teaching jobs if they work on Palestine, but they are routinely paired at academic events on Palestine-Israel with Jewish or Israeli scholars, and rarely given the opportunity to speak in their own right about their own history and ideas. This is, of course, a (settler) colonialist move that erases indigenous knowledge. Palestinian speakers must be accompanied by the presence of Israeli scholars even in spaces supportive of the boycott in order to prove that the boycott is *not* targeting Israeli or Jewish individuals. The constant need to cite the few Israeli scholars who support the boycott performs a similarly paradoxical racial move—that is, the need to disprove the alleged racism of an antiracist campaign (of boycott) by continually highlighting those who continue to enjoy academic and human freedom, and making invisible the bodies that are encaged and disappeared.

Amjad Barham, who is the head of the major Palestinian academic union, the Palestinian Federation of Unions of University Professors and Employees, which was one of the first signatories of the call for BDS, commented in an interview with me:

"Is upholding the academic freedom of Israeli academics a loftier aim than upholding the freedom of an entire people being strangled by an illegal occupation? Do Palestinian universities somehow fall outside the purview of the 'universal' principle of academic freedom? Israeli academics who argue for the protection of their access to international academic networks, grants, visiting professorships, fellowships, and other benefits of the academic system have paid scant attention to the total denial of the most basic freedoms to Palestinians, academics or otherwise." Yet I think the concern with those who have the privilege to exercise their academic freedom, or considered always already deserving of academic freedom, is revealing of the core logic of the academic boycott, that is, a disruption of circuits of academic privilege and academic employment rights that are inherently *racialized*. This is why the academic as well as cultural boycott campaigns have been unsettling for defenders of Israel, both on the left and the right, for they focus on academics and artists— subjects who are ineluctably modern, cosmopolitan, and liberal— as legitimizing a settler colonial state based on racial exclusion. In other words, the academic boycott does not simply take aim at soldiers in combat fatigues (although all Israeli citizens are conscripted into the military, barring Palestinians and orthodox Jews, so academics too do military duty) but concerns the role of subjects in Israel (academics) who supposedly are like *us*. There is a global class identification here that the boycott disrupts, and that makes it deeply discomfiting to those scholars here who believe that the university is not complicit with militarization and racial dispossession here *or* there.

I do not want to discount the vicious attacks on Israeli scholars who support the boycott from within, not to mention Jewish American scholars (as discussed in Chapter 3). However, I do want to illuminate the racial politics of the boycott movement, which has been muddied by an inability, even among progressive U.S. scholars, to have a clearer racial analysis of *Zionism* and thus a more explicit politics of antiracist and anti-Zionist solidarity. As Ilan Pappe, a well-known anti-Zionist Israeli scholar and strong supporter of the boycott, states: "For the few Israelis who sponsored the [BDS] campaign early on, it was a definitive moment that clearly stated our position vis-à-vis the origins, nature, and policies of our state."[26] That is, an ethical stance in support of the boycott clarifies the logic of Zionism as a settler colonial and racist project predicated on the displacement, dispossession, and elimination of the Palestinian population, and leads logically to rejection of that project and refusal of complicity with Israel, through BDS. But Pappe also observes, "I do not regard the moral and active support of Israelis like myself as the most important ingredient in this campaign.... We hope to empower those on the outside who are engaged in the campaign, and we are empowered ourselves by their actions."[27] Thus, the boycott is a form of principled solidarity with Palestinians in their freedom struggle by (Israeli and Jewish) allies who see international pressure as a means to transform a colonial and apartheid condition, which for some is ultimately a brutalization of their own society as well.

Importantly, boycott and BDS organizing outside Palestine has a significant political impact and material effect *in* Palestine and on Palestinian scholars and students, which is why, of course, the latter called for the boycott in the first place. But this point often gets lost in the debate about the academic boycott, which generally focuses on its ramifications for U.S. academics and students. For example, Du'aa (pseudonym), a young Palestinian activist who was a student at Hebrew University, was involved in organizing with other Palestinian youth in Israeli universities against repression, racism, and militarization. She observed, "I believe the [boycott] movement around the world has a big impact on Israeli universities' decisions regarding punishing Palestinian students for protesting within the campuses, and other activities." Palestinian students are regularly punished, disciplined, threatened, and attacked for protesting Israeli wars or being in solidarity with Palestinian prisoners.[28] Du'aa observes that the international pressure generated by BDS campaigns plays an important role in challenging the disciplinary regime of Israeli universities, which have come under increased scrutiny and censure as universities allied with the settler state, not as the democratic and "pluralist" institutions they claim to be.

Samia Botmeh, a Palestinian scholar at Bir Zeit University who has been a member of PACBI's steering committee, observes that academic boycott resolutions in the United States, such as in the ASA, have put "pressure on the Israeli academy, which is the first step in alerting this academy that the world is not going to accept its role in repressing the Palestinians." She adds eloquently: "Undermining the unethical privileged position of the Israeli academy has a tremendous impact on the everyday lives of the Palestinians. The ASA's decision empowers the Palestinians to continue with their struggle against repression and injustice. It helps turn the experience of survival under colonialism to an experience of resistance on the path towards freedom and justice."

The academic and cultural boycott movement and USACBI's campaigns have also had an impact on Palestinian politics and civil society, not just on scholars, students, and cultural workers. Haidar Eid, a PACBI organizer in Gaza, reflected on the ASA resolution:

The impact was huge in Palestine, Gaza in particular, because it became clear that a taboo has been shaken in the U.S.... victories achieved by the academic and cultural boycott movement have drawn the attention of mainstream political organizations and the PA [Palestinian Authority] to the movement, so much so that BDS activists have been asked to hold meetings with political leaders and ministers, including the late Ziyad Abu Ein [who was killed by Israeli soldiers in December 2014], to discuss the best ways of enhancing the BDS campaign.

Similarly, Lisa Taraki points to the role of the boycott in challenging the Oslo paradigm of compromised national politics, as discussed in the Introduction, and the collusion and repression of the PA: "The success of the boycott movement, particularly in the U.S., has had the effect of pushing more and more of Palestinian 'officialdom' (both in the PLO [Palestine Liberation Organization] and the PA) into acknowledging the boycott's great potential in the Palestinian liberation strategy, and adopting some of its tactics. After years of post-Oslo consciousness, this is something that has to be remarked upon." As Taraki suggests, the boycott has ramifications for the Palestinian national struggle and lends support to those in Palestine struggling to revive grassroots resistance after Oslo.

These transformative political shifts on the ground are important to note in response to counterarguments that academic boycott resolutions are simply "symbolic" measures. On the contrary, Botmeh observes, "Palestinian academics and civil society feel empowered by the solidarity expressed by colleagues in associations internationally or individually. This enables us to continue with our everyday lives, which are characterized by extremely harsh conditions, but also strive towards ending oppression through applying pressure on Israel and the

Israeli academy." This is much the same sentiment expressed by South African scholars and artists who also wanted allies to boycott apartheid institutions, and is contrary to claims that it harmed them or was counterproductive.

As Salma Musa (pseudonym), another Palestinian scholar, points out in an important analysis of the Palestinian context for the academic boycott:

> In many ways, BDS reorients our attention to the role that indigenous popular forces, associations, and intellectuals are claiming, outside of both the traditional party framework and a compliant leadership in Palestine, in order to take the decolonial struggle forward, whether in Palestine or in Turtle Island. It is necessary to re-center the histories of anti-colonial struggle that underlie the BDS movement, which have been obfuscated in discussions of BDS. It is often overlooked that many of the Palestinian intellectuals, members of the women's movement, activists and artists which launched the Palestinian Campaign for the Cultural and Academic Boycott of Israel (PACBI) in 2004, or joined the broader BDS movement in 2005, were part of the mass-based movement that led the uprising decades earlier. The fourteen-year period of political organizing that culminated in the *intifada* of 1987 produced popular committees, women's organizations and cooperatives ... that sought to delink native Palestinian society from the Israeli settler colonial system, and build an alternative economy and egalitarian social order.[29]

Musa situates the boycott and BDS within the longer history of Palestinian grassroots resistance and progressive, mass organizing for self-determination, as does Qumsiyeh's research, discussed in Chapter 1; that is, it is not a movement only based in the nonprofit industry.

Furthermore, Musa notes that the BDS movement must be situated in an international genealogy of struggles against colonialism and apartheid, that is, of Third World internationalism.

She highlights linkages with other movements in the global South that inform the paradigm of BDS:

> The BDS movement comes out of and continues the tradition of Third World, decolonial, internationalist struggles. The ways in which the BDS movement has learned from strategies used by the anti-Apartheid struggle in South Africa, and the deep alliances forged with comrades in Brazil and elsewhere have not been taken seriously. In fact, the BDS movement has created a framework for international solidarity that has restored relations between Palestine and other indigenous struggles, Black liberation movements, feminist and LGBT struggles, student movements, and unions, on a scale not seen since the 1970s when the PLO allied with movements across the global south.[30]

The boycott, and the BDS movement at large, provides a framework for antiracist solidarity that also challenges anti-Blackness in the United States, as observed by BDS organizer Kristian Bailey, who has been active in the Palestine solidarity movement since he was a student. Bailey has been engaged in various campaigns that link incarceration, policing, and securitization in the United States and Palestine-Israel. He argues that one of the underlying principles of this transnational organizing is applying "the right of return locally and globally. One of the best ways to ensure return is possible for Palestinians is to reverse the process of colonization of indigenous land and cycles of displacement for working class, Black, and brown people in our own colonized territory."[31] Bailey, who is one of the leaders of the Blacks4Palestine campaign, offers an analysis that counters the charges that the boycott or BDS movement devalues Black lives, or is somehow even anti-Black.[32] This is not to presume that there is no anti-Black racism within the boycott movement or that its racial politics is above criticism; no movement is politically pure and without its problems and internal contradictions. Robin Kelley has offered the most incisive commentary on the debate about anti-Blackness and BDS: "Black/Palestinian solidarity—like any solidarity—ought to be understood as a political project rather than some kind of natural alliance. There was never a time when the vast majority of Black people supported the right of Palestinians to self-determination or criticized Israeli policy, or when the vast majority of Palestinians—either in the Occupied Territories, in '48 Palestine, or living in exile, actively supported Black liberation."[33]

Kelley, who himself has written about Black Zionism in the first half of the twentieth century, as discussed in Chapter 1, provides a thoughtful conceptualization of solidarity and antiracist politics: "Solidarity is a political stance, not a racial imperative. Solidarities are often fragile, temporary, and always forged and sustained in struggle. Solidarity can produce internal fracturing within groups, sharp disagreements, and new alliances because it is constituted historically, in real places, times, and conditions. And no solidarity based on 'identity' of any kind can achieve unanimity—that is to say, anti-Black racism does not produce a united, uniform, unanimous Black anti-racist response, nor do the depredations of Israeli settler colonialism produce a similarly unified Palestinian response."[34] There is clearly room for developing deeper frameworks of antiracist solidarity in the boycott and BDS movement, which it must be noted emerged just thirteen years ago. But as Bailey, echoing Musa's view, states of the call for boycott: "It is fully within the realm of this call to use BDS as a stepping stone in the fight for both Palestinian self-determination and local freedom."[35]

The decolonial and internationalist impetus for the BDS and boycott movement does not mean that global solidarity and grassroots resistance outside Palestine should displace Palestinian-led struggles, in Palestine or in the diaspora. On the contrary, as Musa observes, "the BDS movement has made clear that it is not a replacement for the PLO or a democratically elected national body representing the Palestinian people. Whether to rebuild the PLO or replace it with another national body is an internal discussion Palestinians are having."[36] In a similar refrain, Jordy Rosenberg says, "I think the future of the boycott movement is going to be determined—as it has always been—by those who are most directly affected by Zionist colonialism ... as the BDS movement will continue to be inspired by Palestinian calls for solidarity." These activists underscore that the BDS movement is ultimately in support of Palestinian self-determination, even as it expresses a principled form of solidarity that Palestinians have called for from the international community. Indeed, the relentless assaults by Israel on Palestinians in Gaza, the West Bank, and Jerusalem, as well as continued and intensified repression of Palestinians inside Israel, has been accompanied by growing BDS organizing in Palestine and increased coordination internationally with campaigns across the world, as well as an even sharper analysis of the role of BDS in popular resistance in Palestine, based on a unified Palestinian national collective across colonial borders and in the diaspora.[37]

CONCLUSION

The academic boycott movement has exposed the materiality of the links between the U.S. and Israeli state and academic institutions and the forces that have upheld this collusion, pitting U.S. academics against Palestinian scholars and students and the Palestinian people at large. The boycott transforms this colonial relationship, based on racial hierarchy and racial privilege, into a refusal of complicity with colonialism and apartheid, and into cross-racial, transnational solidarity. Salaita describes the BDS movement as "a site of principled decolonial activity, and subsequently as something that must oppose any disparity of power based on class, race, gender, religion, sexuality, culture, and nationality."[38] As in all anticolonial struggles, cultural and intellectual decolonization is key to liberation for the oppressed, not just political liberation from colonial rule. In focusing on the academy, the boycott has become part of a struggle for the radical decolonization of knowledge, or epistemic decolonization, including from the shackles of Zionist and U.S. settler colonialism, and is thus a productive new site of knowledge production erupting within the settler university.

The boycott has also been accompanied by proactive efforts to enhance academic freedom for Palestinians and promote Palestinian decolonial thought. It has led to a plethora of academic panels, a slew of publications in both academic and nonacademic venues, numerous talks, and countless conversations about what freedom and un-freedom in Palestine, as well as in the United States, means. For example, Rajini Srikanth, who is at the University of Massachusetts–Boston, says: "On my campus, I am part of the group 'Faculty and Staff for Justice in Palestine.' Our group supports proboycott efforts locally, regionally, and nationally. We are currently in the process of developing a course on Israel/Palestine for the human rights minor on our campus." Thus, acts of refusal that are at the core of the boycott strategy also occur in tandem with positive efforts to produce critical knowledge about Palestine, Israel, and settler colonialism.

The campaigns for boycott analyzed in this book demonstrate a tidal shift in knowledge production and discourse about Palestine since the call for academic and cultural boycott in 2004, the formation of USACBI in 2009, and the spread of boycott organizing across the United States in recent years, in parallel with the rapidly expanding divestment movement in colleges, churches, unions, and local communities. Lisa Rofel observes, "What is significant about social movements is their slow, steady building of coalitions that create change." From a small, motley group of scholars and activists, USACBI has grown and spawned national boycott campaigns that rocked the U.S. establishment and alerted Zionist leaders that change had come. Bill Mullen reflects on the future of the boycott movement by invoking

> the opening line of Ali Abunimah's great book *The Battle for Justice in Palestine.* He begins by saying, "The Palestinians are winning." He means that despite the horrific and brutal conditions for Palestinians under occupation, BDS has helped to shift public discourse in the West towards sympathy with the Palestinians. Polls now show that support for Palestinians has increased from 9 percent to 27 percent among "millennials" in the U.S. just in the past few years. In 2016 alone, sixteen new boycott or divestment resolutions have been passed in the U.S. Internationally, the E.U. has agreed to label goods produced in Israeli settlements as a response to pressure from BDS activists. In this year's presidential election, while Hillary Clinton and Donald Trump have been predictably awful and reactionary in expressing support for Israel, Bernie Sanders appointed Cornel West to be a delegate to the Democratic Party platform committee, where he tried valiantly to get the party to include the words "occupation" and "apartheid." Jill Stein has endorsed BDS ... as the Green Party candidate for president. All of these are victories generated by the BDS movement.

Indeed, the 2016 U.S. presidential election and Trump's victory spurred more vigorous and vocal progressive mobilization on campuses and in communities, with solidarity campaigns binding together movements against police violence and militarization, and for racial justice, immigrant rights and sanctuary, gender and sexual rights, indigenous sovereignty, environmental justice, and freedom in Palestine. The historic Women's March in January 2017, which mobilized masses of people to come out in the streets against Trump after his inauguration, was called for by prominent feminist activists such as Angela Davis and Palestinian American Linda Sarsour, who have advocated for BDS as part of a feminist politics. The International Women's Strike on March 8, 2017, explicitly included a call for "the decolonization of Palestine" in its platform, and for the dismantling of "all walls, from prison walls to border walls, from Mexico to Palestine."[39] These campaigns build on the solidarities that were created in previous years as the BDS movement made linkages with Black Lives Matter, the antiwar and prison abolition movement, labor unions, faith-based activists, and feminist and queer groups. As "White supremacy" became a term permissible in discussions on major cable news networks about Trump and his alt-right followers, there were also growing conversations about Zionism, the ways it can become imbricated with anti-Semitism on the right, and the need to challenge racial supremacy and White privilege. Palestine has become central to all of these major contemporary debates and resistance movements. Omar Barghouti writes about the struggle for liberation, equality, and dignity waged through BDS:

> The global BDS movement for Palestinian rights presents a progressive, antiracist, sophisticated, sustainable, moral, and effective form of nonviolent civil resistance. It has become one of the key political catalysts and moral anchors for a strengthened, reinvigorated international social movement capable of ending the law of the jungle and upholding in its stead the rule of law, reaffirming the rights of all humans to freedom, equality, and dignified living.
> Our South Africa moment has finally arrived![40]

There really is no turning back.

I will end by paying homage to the Palestinians who have been waging their struggle for liberation for over seventy years, and who have been engaging in acts of resistance and boycott against colonialism and foreign rule for much longer. They do so along with many other subjugated peoples around the world, and the boycott movement emerges from this deep interconnectedness of freedom struggles. The growth of the boycott movement, as I have documented in this book, has been partly fueled by Israel's ongoing aggression and violence and by the outrage of people who feel they can no longer be silent, but must act. We actually pay a relatively very small price for our boycott work and solidarity activism in the United States. I recognize that the victories of the boycott and BDS movement emerge from a painful history of loss, including loss of (Palestinian) lives, but also from the steadfast desire of Palestinians, and others, to be free. If Palestinians can be resilient under these conditions and remain steadfast, practicing *sumuud,* so must we.

ACKNOWLEDGMENTS

I am incredibly grateful to Lisa Duggan and Curtis Marez for their vision in editing this series, and for inviting me to write about the academic boycott movement. Their principled and courageous leadership of the American Studies Association is integral to the story that I tell in this book, and is part of the historic shift in the U.S. academy that I document here. Thank you, Niels Hooper, for your amazing support and for the opportunity to work on this book! I also am indebted to Marez and Alex Lubin as well as the anonymous reviewer for wonderful feedback. Thanks to Bradley Depew, Renee Donovan, and Kate Hoffman for shepherding this project through the process of becoming a book. I appreciate Jeff Wyneken's meticulous and speedy work with the copyediting.

I'd like to give a shout-out to all my fellow organizers in USACBI (US Campaign for the Academic and Cultural Boycott of Israel), and to our colleagues in PACBI (Palestinian Campaign for the Academic and Cultural Boycott of Israel). Their work has fundamentally altered the political terrain, and there are also many more who remain unnamed from the BDS movement, who have organized for years with little reward and often at great cost to them and their careers.

Lastly, this book is dedicated to the fugitive scholars who refused to remain silent and had to go into exile: you know who you are, and your courage will not be forgotten.

NOTES

INTRODUCTION

1. http://pacbi.org/etemplate.php?id = 869.

2. https://bdsmovement.net/what-is-bds.

3. https://bdsmovement.net/what-is-bds.

4. For example, Omar Barghouti, *BDS-Boycott, Divestment, and Sanctions: The Global Struggle for Palestinian Rights* (Chicago: Haymarket, 2011); Audrea Lim, ed., *The Case for Sanctions against Israel* (London: Verso, 2012); Ashley Dawson and Bill Mullen, eds., *Against Apartheid: The Case for Boycotting Israeli Universities* (Chicago: Haymarket, 2015).

5. See Sam Ramsamy, *Apartheid: The Real Hurdle—Sport in South Africa and the International Boycott* (London: International Defence and Aid Fund for Southern Africa, 1982).

6. Omar Barghouti, "The Academic Boycott of Israel: Reaching a Tipping Point?," in Dawson and Mullen, *Against Apartheid*, 60.

7. http://right2edu.birzeit.edu/.

8. At www.usacbi.org/mission-statement/.

9. George Giacaman and Dag J. Lonning, eds., *After Oslo: New Realities, Old Problems* (London: Pluto Press, 1998).

10. Cited in Sherene Seikaly and Noura Erekat, "Tahrir's Other Sky," in *The Dawn of the Arab Uprisings: End of an Old Order?* edited by

Bassam Haddad, Rosie Bsheer, and Ziad Abu-Rish (London: Pluto Press, 2012), 275.

11. Sari Hanafi and Linda Tabar, "The Intifada and the Aid Industry: The Impact of the New Liberal Agenda on the Palestinian NGOs," *Comparative Studies of South Asia, Africa, and the Middle East* 23, nos. 1–2 (2003): 205–14.

12. Named after the areas in apartheid South Africa in which Blacks were confined by forced removal as part of the Bantustan (or "homeland") policy.

13. Sunaina Maira, *Jil Oslo: Palestinian Hip Hop, Youth Culture, and the Youth Movement* (Tadween, 2013).

14. Lori Allen, *The Rise and Fall of Human Rights: Cynicism and Politics in Occupied Palestine* (Stanford, CA: Stanford University Press, 2013).

15. See the *Social Text/Periscope* special issue on the academic boycott movement for more on this: http://socialtextjournal.org /periscope_topic/the-academic-boycott-movement/.

16. Allen, *Rise and Fall of Human Rights*.

17. Jacques Rancière, *Dissensus: On Politics and Aesthetics*, edited and translated by Steven Corcoran (London: Continuum, 2010), 38. Electronic edition.

18. Sunaina Maira, "A Radical Vision of Freedom," in "The Academic Boycott Movement," special issue of *Periscope/Social Text*, November 2016, http://socialtextjournal.org/periscope_article/a-radical-vision-of-freedom/.

19. Maira, "Academic Boycott Movement."

20. Steven Salaita, *Inter/nationalism: Decolonizing Native America and Palestine* (Minneapolis: University of Minnesota Press, 2016), 35.

CHAPTER ONE. BOYCOTT AS TACTIC

1. Manning Marable, *Race, Reform, and Rebellion: The Second Reconstruction in Black America, 1945–2006*, 3rd. ed. (Jackson: University Press of Mississippi, 2007), 40.

2. Clayborne Carson, *In Struggle: SNCC and the Black Awakening of the 1960s* (Cambridge: Harvard University Press, 1995 ed.), 44.

3. Marable, *Race, Reform, and Rebellion*, 40.

4. Ibid.

5. Ibid., 20.

6. Ibid., 24.

7. Cited in Clayborne Carson et al., eds., *The Eyes on the Prize Civil Rights Reader: Documents, Speeches, and Firsthand Accounts from the Black Freedom Struggle* (New York: Penguin, 1991), 49.

8. Cited in ibid., 154.

9. Carson, *In Struggle*, 4.

10. Ibid., 4.

11. Ibid., 11.

12. See the Kairos document at www.kairospalestine.ps/index.php/about-us/kairos-palestine-document.

13. Marable, *Race, Reform, and Rebellion*, 74.

14. Cited in Carson et al., *Eyes on the Prize*, 157.

15. For some examples of this criticism of BDS, see Ali Abunimah, "Finkelstein Renews Attack on BDS 'Cult,'" *Electronic Intifada*, June 4, 2012, https://electronicintifada.net/blogs/ali-abunimah/finkelstein-renews-attack-bds-cult-calls-palestinians-who-pursue-their-rights; Noam Chomsky, "On Israel-Palestine and BDS," *The Nation*, July 2, 2014, www.thenation.com/article/israel-palestine-and-bds/.

16. Ibid.

17. Marable, *Race, Reform, and Rebellion*; Alex Lubin, *Geographies of Liberation: The Making of an Afro-Arab Political Imaginary* (Chapel Hill: University of North Carolina Press, 2014); Marjorie Feld, *Nations Divided: American Jews and the Struggle over Apartheid* (London: Palgrave Macmillan, 2014).

18. Feld, *Nations Divided*, 44.

19. Ibid., 69.

20. Robin Kelley, "Apartheid's Black Apologists," in *Apartheid Israel: The Politics of an Analogy*, edited by Jon Soske and Sean Jacobs, 2014, https://africaisacountry.atavist.com/apartheidanalogy.

21. Ibid.

22. Cited in Feld, *Nations Divided*, 65.

23. Ibid., 43.

24. Ibid.

25. Ibid., III.

26. Heidi Grunebaum, "Through the Looking Glass: From South Africa to Israel/Palestine and Back Again," in Soske and Jacobs, *Apartheid Israel*.

27. Salim Vally, "From South Africa: Solidarity with Palestine," in Soske and Jacobs, *Apartheid Israel*.

28. Cited in Ben White, *Israeli Apartheid: A Beginner's Guide* (London: Pluto Press, 2009), 3; Ashley Dawson and Bill V. Mullen, *Against Apartheid: The Case for Boycotting Israeli Universities* (Chicago: Haymarket, 2015), 2. These include racialized restrictions on "the right to life and liberty," "the right to leave and to return to their country, the right to a nationality, the right to freedom of movement and residence," as well as the "creation of separate reserves and ghettos for members of a racial group or groups" and the "expropriation of landed property belonging to a racial group." In 1988, the Rome Statute of the International Criminal Court listed apartheid as one of the "crimes against humanity" (White, *Israeli Apartheid*, 4–5).

29. Dawson and Mullen, *Against Apartheid*, 3–4.

30. Ibid., 4–5.

31. Ibid., 3.

32. White, *Israeli Apartheid*, 8. See also T.J. Tallie, "The Historian of Apartheid," in Soske and Jacobs, *Apartheid Israel*.

33. "Tutu Condemns Israeli Apartheid," *BBC News*, April 29, 2002, http://news.bbc.co.uk/2/hi/africa/1957644.stm.

34. Jimmy Carter, *Palestine: Peace Not Apartheid* (New York: Simon & Schuster, 2006).

35. Salim Vally, "Palestinian Solidarity in South Africa and the Academic Boycott of Israel," in Dawson and Mullen, *Against Apartheid*, 95.

36. Cited in Salim Vally, "From South Africa: Solidarity with Palestine," in Soske and Jacobs, *Apartheid Israel*.

37. Vally, "Palestinian Solidarity," 95.

38. Keith Feldman, *A Shadow over Palestine: The Imperial Life of Race in America* (Minneapolis: University of Minnesota Press, 2015); Nada Elia,

"The Burden of Representation," in *Arab and Arab American Feminisms: Gender, Violence and Belonging,* edited by Rabab Abdulhadi, Evelyn Alsultany, and Nadine Naber (Syracuse, NY: Syracuse University Press, 2011), 141–58.

39. Cited in Feld, *Nations Divided,* 98.

40. Matt Garcia, *From the Jaws of Victory: The Triumph and Tragedy of Cesar Chavez and the Farmworker Movement* (Berkeley: University of California Press, 2012), 62.

41. Ibid., 7.

42. Ben Norton, "California Leads the Way in the Block the Boat Movement," *Mondoweiss,* October 2014, http://mondoweiss.net/2014/10 /california-block-movement/amp/.

43. Lara Kiswani, "Why We Are Blocking the Boat," *Mondoweiss,* October 2014, http://mondoweiss.net/2014/10/blocking-the-boat/amp/.

44. Garcia, *From the Jaws of Victory,* 7.

45. Ibid., 59–60.

46. Antonio Gramsci, *Selections from the Prison Notebooks,* edited and translated by Quintin Hoare and Geoffrey N. Smith (New York: International Publishers, 1997), 108–14, 238–39.

47. Philip Weiss, "Israel Lobby Panics," *Mondoweiss,* August 6, 2016, http://mondoweiss.net/2016/08/generation-american-leaders/.

48. Cited in Garcia, *From the Jaws of Victory,* 73.

49. Curtis Marez, *Farmworker Futurism: Speculative Technologies of Resistance* (Minneapolis: University of Minnesota Press, 2016), 96.

50. Ibid.

51. Ibid., 107.

52. Garcia, *From the Jaws of Victory,* 296.

53. Omar Barghouti, *BDS-Boycott, Divestment, and Sanctions: The Global Struggle for Palestinian Rights* (Chicago: Haymarket, 2011), 225.

54. Edward W. Said, *Orientalism* [1978] (New York: Random House/ Vintage, 1981 ed.).

55. Mazin Qumsiyeh, *Popular Resistance in Palestine: A History of Hope and Empowerment* (London: Pluto Press, 2011).

56. Ibid., 11.

57. Ibid., 36–43.

58. Ibid., 64–65.

59. Cited in ibid., 73.

60. Ibid., 80.

61. Ibid.

62. Ibid., 84–85.

63. Ibid., 138.

64. Magid Shihade, *Not Just a Soccer Game: Colonialism and Conflict among Palestinians in Israel* (Syracuse, NY: Syracuse University Press, 2011).

65. Qumsiyeh, *Popular Resistance in Palestine,* 141.

66. Cited in ibid., 151–52.

67. Amer Shomali and Paul Cowan, dirs., *The Wanted 18,* 2014, www .wanted18.com/.

68. Cited in Qumsiyeh, *Popular Resistance in Palestine,* 150.

69. Clayborne Carson, *In Struggle: SNCC and the Black Awakening of the 1960s* (Cambridge: Harvard University Press, 1995).

CHAPTER TWO. THE ACADEMIC BOYCOTT MOVEMENT

1. See www.usacbi.org.

2. See https://bdsmovement.net/pacbi.

3. See statistic sheet at "US Military Aid and the Israel-Palestine Conflict," http://ifamericansknew.org/stat/usaid.html. In September 2016, the Obama administration offered Israel the largest military aid package in U.S. history, about $38 billion over ten years; despite perceived tensions between Obama and Israeli prime minister Benjamin Netanyahu, the "special relationship" between Israel and the United States was stronger than ever ("Largest-ever Military Aid Package to Go to Israel," *CNN,* September 13, 2016, www.cnn.com/2016/09/13 /politics/us-israel-military-aid-package-mou/).

4. "Marking Day of Solidarity, Ban Calls for Easing Hardship of Palestinians," *UN News Centre,* November 24, 2008, www.un.org/apps /news/story.asp?NewsID=29056&Cr=palestin&Cr1#.WaeoypMrLow.

5. Ibid.

6. Thalif Deen, "UN Assembly Head Hailed for Slamming Israel," *Electronic Intifada,* December 3, 2008, https://electronicintifada.net/content/un-assembly-head-hailed-slamming-israel/7841.

7. Mazin Qumsiyeh, *Popular Resistance in Palestine: A History of Hope and Empowerment* (London: Pluto Press, 2011), 214.

8. www.usacbi.org/about/.

9. www.usacbi.org/advisory-board/.

10. See the ASA resolution at www.theasa.net/american_studies_association_resolution_on_academic_boycott_of_israel.

11. http://aaastudies.org/wp-content/uploads/2014/12/aaas-4_20_13-conference-resolution-to-support-the-boycott-of-israeli-academic-institutions.pdf.

12. See the resolution at www.humanist-sociology.org/about1-cx2j.

13. See www.usacbi.org/academic-associations-endorsing-boycott/.

14. Ibid.

15. See the resolution at www.pacbi.org/etemplate.php?id=2319.

16. See http://socialtextjournal.org/periscope_article/529-2/.

17. http://socialtextjournal.org/periscope_topic/palestine/.

18. http://socialtextjournal.org/periscope_article/statement-of-usacbi-delegation-to-palestine/.

19. http://socialtextjournal.org/periscope_article/statement-of-usacbi-delegation-to-palestine/.

20. http://socialtextjournal.org/periscope_article/statement-of-usacbi-delegation-to-palestine/.

21. http://mondoweiss.net/2012/02/a-level-of-racist-violence-i-have-never-seen-ucla-professor-robin-d-g-kelley-on-palestine-and-the-bds-movement/.

22. Robin D.G. Kelley, "Normalized Supremacy, Dignifying Resistance," *Social Text/Periscope,* July 2012, http://socialtextjournal.org/periscope_article/normalized_supremacy_dignifying_resistance/.

23. Robin Kelley, interview with Alex Kane, "A Level of Racist Violence I Have Never Seen," *Mondoweiss,* February 16, 2012, http://mondoweiss.net/2012/02/a-level-of-racist-violence-i-have-never-seen-ucla-professor-robin-d-g-kelley-on-palestine-and-the-bds-movement/.

24. J. Kehaulani Kauanui, "One Occupation," *Social Text/ Periscope*, July 5, 2012, http://socialtextjournal.org/periscope_article /one_occupation/.

25. Some of the talks presented are published at www.jadaliyya .com/pages/index/15697/substantive-erasures_essays-on-academic-boycott-an.

26. https://electronicintifada.net/content/taboo-boycotting-israel-has-been-broken/12949.

27. Alex Lubin, "Breaking 'America's Last Taboo,'" *Middle East Research and Information Project*, November 27, 2013, www.merip.org/breaking-%E2%80%9Camerica%E2%80%99s-last-taboo%E2%80%9D.

28. For example, see the essays in *Borderlands* 14, no. 1, a special issue on "The Politics of Suffering" (2015), edited by Nadera Shalhoub-Kevorkian: www.borderlands.net.au/issues/vol14no1.html.

29. See David Palumbo-Liu, "Millennials Are Over Israel," *Salon*, August 1, 2014, www.salon.com/2014/08/01/millennials_are_so_over_israel_a_new_generation_is_outraged_over_gaza_demands_change/.

30. Edward Said, "America's Last Taboo," *New Left Review* 6 (November/December 2000): 45–53.

31. www.theasa.net/american_studies_association_resolution_on_academic_boycott_of_israel.

32. Ibid.

33. David Lloyd and Malini J. Schuller, "The Israeli State of Exception and the Case for Academic Boycott," in *Against Apartheid: The Case for Boycotting Israeli Universities*, edited by Ashley Dawson and Bill V. Mullen (Chicago: Haymarket, 2015), 68.

34. Ibid., 71.

35. See www.usacbi.org/academic-associations-endorsing-boycott/.

36. https://docs.google.com/document/d/1rwcBy3NQIK4SiFD6hERrg-WMK6L_swwVBtZbjnPQLFg/edit.

37. https://anthroboycott.wordpress.com/2016/06/07/the-struggle-continues-campaign-for-boycott-of-israeli-academic-institutions-undeterred.

38. www.merip.org/breaking-%E2%80%9Camerica%E2%80%99s-last-taboo%E2%80%9D.

39. www.dreamdefenders.org/ddpalestine.

40. See Nora Barrows-Friedman, *In Our Power: US Students Organize for Justice in Palestine* (Charlottesville, VA: Just World, 2014).

41. Ibid., 38; Sunaina M. Maira, *The 9/11 Generation: Youth, Rights, and Solidarity in the War on Terror* (New York: NYU Press, 2016).

42. Lena Ibrahim, "What Happened There Was Historic," *Mondoweiss,* November 27, 2013, http://mondoweiss.net/2013/11/happened-american-association/.

43. Ibid.

CHAPTER THREE. BACKLASH

1. Cited in Omar Barghouti, "The Academic Boycott of Israel: Reaching a Tipping Point?," in *Against Apartheid: The Case for Boycotting Israeli Universities,* edited by Ashley Dawson and Bill V. Mullen (Chicago: Haymarket, 2015), 56.

2. Reut Institute, "Contending with BDS and the Assault on Israel's Legitimacy," June 25, 2015, http://reut-institute.org/Publication .aspx?PublicationId=4224.

3. See https://electronicintifada.net/content/behind-brand-israel-israels-recent-propaganda-efforts/8694.

4. Ibid.

5. For example, Reut Institute, "Eroding Israel's Legitimacy in the International Arena," January 28, 2010, http://reut-institute.org /Publication.aspx?PublicationId=3766.

6. Cited in Barghouti, "Academic Boycott," 55.

7. Ibid., 57.

8. http://mondoweiss.net/2011/03/university-of-johannesburg-to-officially-severed-ties-with-israel%E2%80%99s-ben-gurion-university/. See Salim Vally, "Palestinian Solidarity in South Africa and the Academic Boycott of Israel: The Case of the University of Johannesburg and Ben Gurion University," in Dawson and Mullen, *Against Apartheid.*

9. Barghouti, "Academic Boycott," p. 57.

10. "Netanyahu Government Ramps Up Efforts to Combat BDS," *Mondoweiss,* June 8, 2015, http://mondoweiss.net/2015/06/netanyahu-government-combat/.

11. This was the title of the working paper for the Herzilya Conference in Israel in 2010; see https://electronicintifada.net/content/behind-brand-israel-israels-recent-propaganda-efforts/8694.

12. Ali Abunimah, *The Battle for Justice in Palestine* (Chicago: Haymarket Books, 2014), 171.

13. Achille Mmembe, "Necropolitics," translated by Libby Meintjes, *Public Culture* 15, no. 1 (2003): 11–40.

14. Itamar Eichner, "Israel to Allocate NIS 100 Shekel for BDS Battle," *Y-Net News,* July 6, 2015, www.ynetnews.com/articles/0,7340,L-4665676,00.html.

15. See David Lloyd and Malini J. Schuller, "The Israeli State of Exception and the Case for Academic Boycott," in Dawson and Mullen, *Against Apartheid,* 65–72.

16. Abunimah, *Battle for Justice in Palestine,* 180.

17. International Jewish Anti-Zionist Network, *The Business of Backlash: The Attack on the Palestinian Movement and Other Movements for Social Justice,*2015,www.ijan.org/wp-content/uploads/2015/04/IJAN-Business-of-Backlash-Executive-Summary-web1.pdf.

18. International Jewish Anti-Zionist Network, *Business of Backlash,* 8.

19. Ibid., 9.

20. See https://theintercept.com/2016/05/13/interview-with-bds-advocate-omar-barghouti-banned-by-israel-from-traveling-threatened-with-worse/.

21. Max Ajl, "Academic Freedom Controversy Brewing at University of California," *Electronic Intifada,* May 20, 2009, http://electronicintifada.net/content/academic-freedom-controversy-brewing-university-california/8242.

22. Ali Abunimah, "New York Times Ad Including BDS Movement, College Professors of Inciting Murder of Jewish Children," *Electronic Intifada,* April 24, 2012, https://electronicintifada.net/blogs/ali-abunimah/new-york-times-ad-accuses-bds-movement-college-professors-inciting-murder-jewish.

23. www.amchainitiative.org/antisemitism-tracker.

24. "The Top Ten Anti-Israel Groups in America," posted at Anti-Defamation League on October 4, 2010, www.adl.org/main_

Anti_Israel/top_ten_anti_israel_groups.htm?Multi_page_sections= sHeading_2.

25. See Steven Salaita, *Israel's Dead Soul* (Philadelphia: Temple University Press, 2011).

26. Ibid., 14.

27. Ibid., 41.

28. Abunimah, *Battle for Justice in Palestine*, 185.

29. International Jewish Anti-Zionist Network, *Business of Backlash*, www.ijan.org/resources/business-of-backlash/.

30. Abunimah, *Battle for Justice in Palestine*, 213.

31. See www.blackforpalestine.com/.

32. www.usacbi.org/2015/11/new-video-prominent-artists-call-for-cultural-boycott-of-israel/.

33. See https://policy.m4bl.org/about/.

34. See https://pqbds.wordpress.com/.

35. See the eloquent letter written in response by Robin Kelley: http://mondoweiss.net/2013/06/letter-refugee-camp/.

36. Robin Kelley, "Apartheid's Black Apologists," in *Apartheid Israel: The Politics of an Analogy*, 2014, https://africaisacountry.atavist.com /apartheidanalogy.

37. Gale C. Toensing, "Redwashing Panel Follows Academic Associations' Boycott of Israel," *Indian Country Today Media Network*, December 13, 2013, http://indiancountrytodaymedianetwork.com/2013 /12/31/redwashing-panel-follows-academic-associations-boycott-israel-152930.

38. One of the most vociferous and belligerent redwashing activists is Ryan Bellerose, an indigenous Canadian and self-described Zionist who belongs to Calgary United with Israel; see http://indiancountry todaymedianetwork.com/2014/01/11/dont-mix-indigenous-fight-palestinian-rights?page=1.

39. For example, www.insidehighered.com/views/2014/08/08/essay-defends-university-illinois-decision-not-hire-steven-salaita.

40. Lloyd and Schuller, "Israeli State of Exception," 68–69. See the special issue at www.aaup.org/reports-publications/journal-academic-freedom/volume-4.

41. Lloyd and Schuller, "Israeli State of Exception," 69.

42. Salaita, *Israel's Dead Soul.*

43. Peter Beinart, "To Save Israel, Boycott the Settlements," *New York Times,* March 18, 2012, www.nytimes.com/2012/03/19/opinion/to-save-israel-boycott-the-settlements.html.

44. Taly Krupkin, "Israel's Travel Ban Backlash: Over 100 Jewish Studies Scholars Threaten to Not Visit Israel in Protest," *Haaretz,* March 10, 2017, www.haaretz.com/us-news/.premium-1.776373.

45. Steven Levitsky and Glen Weyl, "We Are Lifelong Zionists: Here's Why We've Chosen to Boycott Israel," *Washington Post,* October 23, 2015, www.washingtonpost.com/opinions/a-zionist-case-for-boycotting-israel/2015/10/23/ac4dab80–735c-11e5–9cbb-790369643cf9_story.html?tid=a_inl&utm_term=.155a081906b1.

46. Anti-Defamation League, "ADL and Reut Institute Forge New Joint Initiative to Battle BDS and the Delegimitization of Israel," February 29, 2016, www.adl.org/press-center/press-releases/israel-middle-east/adl-and-reut-institute-forge-new-joint-initiative-battle-bds-delegitimization.html.

47. See www.frontpagemag.com/fpm/262586/horowitz-defends-anti-bds-poster-campaign-charges-sara-dogan; Wilson Dizard, "New Campaign Uses Racist Posters to Target Palestinian Campus Activists by Name," *Mondoweiss,* October 27, 2016, http://mondoweiss.net/2016/10/campaign-palestinian-activists/; see the powerful response by Jerry Kang, UCLA's Vice Chancellor for Equity, Diversity, and Inclusion, April 19, 2016, http://jerrykang.net/wp-content/blogs.dir/1/files/2016/04/Crosscheck-2016–04–19-Dialogue-over-Demagoguery.pdf.

48. Alex Lubin, "Breaking 'America's Last Taboo,'" www.merip.org/breaking-%E2%80%9Camerica%E2%80%99s-last-taboo%E2%80%9D.

49. Jasbir Puar, *Terrorist Assemblages: Homonationalism in Queer Times* (Durham, NC: Duke University Press, 2007), 45.

50. Nora Barrows-Friedman, "Bogus Allegations of 'Anti-Semitism' Create Real Climate of Fear for Arab, Muslim Students in US," *Electronic Intifada,* August 8, 2012, http://electronicintifada.net/content/bogus-allegations-anti-semitism-create-real-climate-fear-arab-muslim-students-us/11563; Yaman Salahi, "The Echo Chamber of

Campus Anti-Semitism," *Al Jazeera*, August 29, 2012, www.aljazeera .com/indepth/opinion/2012/08/201282991348710688.html.

51. See Nora Barrows-Friedman, "Victory for Campus Free Speech as US Dept of Education Throws Out Anti-Semitism Complaints," *Electronic Intifada*, August 28, 2013, http://electronicintifada .net/blogs/nora-barrows-friedman/victory-campus-free-speech-us-dept-education-throws-out-anti-semitism.

52. Nora Barrows-Friedman, *In Our Power: U.S. Students Organize for Justice in Palestine* (Charlottesville, VA: Just World, 2014), 98.

53. Abunimah, *Battle for Justice in Palestine*, 186.

54. Ibid., 193. The text of the resolution, which was opposed by the UC Student Association, is at http://leginfo.legislature.ca.gov/faces /billTextClient.xhtml;jsessionid=d4df7d3510900146efbbc88f1045?bill_ id=201120120HR35.

55. Abunimah, *Battle for Justice in Palestine*, 171.

56. http://palestinelegal.org/the-palestine-exception.

57. Cited in Samantha Brotman, "Salaita Speaks Out, Warns of a Palestinian Exception to the First Amendment and Academic Freedom," *Mondoweiss*, September 10, 2014, http://mondoweiss.net/2014/09 /palestinian-exception-amendment.

58. Ali Abunimah, "Climate of Fear Silencing Palestinian, Muslim Students at UC Campuses, Rights Groups Warn," *Electronic Intifada*, December 4, 2012, http://electronicintifada.net/blogs/ali-abunimah /climate-fear-silencing-palestinian-muslim-students-university-california-rights.

59. See the statement by the Department of Education's Office of Civil Rights dismissing the complaint against UC Berkeley: http:// newscenter.berkeley.edu/wp-content/uploads/2013/08/DOE.OCR_.pdf.

60. See the report by Palestine Solidarity Legal Support, "The Systematic Attempt to Shut Down Student Speech at the University of California," http://palestinelegalsupport.org/download/advocacy-documents/FACT%20SHEET%20Shutting%20Down%20Student% 20Speech%20at%20U.C._fn_DISTRIBUTE.pdf.

61. www.insidehighered.com/views/2013/05/20/asian-american-studies-professor-responds-israel-boycott.

62. www.state.gov/j/drl/rls/fs/2010/122352.htm.

63. http://regents.universityofcalifornia.edu/aar/mare.pdf.

64. See UC faculty letter circulated by JVP: https://jewishvoice-forpeace.org/uc-faculty-letter-to-regents/.

65. See www.usacbi.org/2016/04/usacbi-statement-on-uc-regents-principles-challenging-racism-means-challenging-zionism/.

66. See Piya Chatterjee and Sunaina Maira, eds., "Introduction," in *The Imperial University: Academic Repression and Scholarly Dissent* (Minneapolis: University of Minnesota Press, 2014).

67. Lisa Taraki, in Omar Barghouti, Rema Hammami, Sondra Hale, Hilary Rose, and Lisa Taraki, "Critics of the AAUP Report," *Academe* 92, no. 5 (September–October 2006): 56.

68. Omar Barghouti, in Barghouti et al., 44; Judith Butler, "Israel/Palestine and the Paradoxes of Academic Freedom," *Radical Philosophy* 135 (January–February 2006): 8–17.

69. Magid Shihade, "The Academic Boycott of Israel and Its Critics," in Dawson and Mullen, *Against Apartheid*, 50.

70. Ibid.

71. Ibid., 48. Emphasis mine.

72. Randall Williams, *The Divided World: Human Rights and Its Violence* (Minneapolis: University of Minnesota Press, 2010).

73. The AAUP called for divestment from corporations complicit with apartheid South Africa in 1985, and acknowledges that this was a "form of boycott," if not an academic boycott as such. Joan W. Scott et al., "On Academic Boycotts," www.aaup.org/report/academic-boycotts.

74. http://palestinelegal.org/the-palestine-exception.

75. See Campus Defense Coalition for Palestine, https://cdc4p .wordpress.com/.

CHAPTER FOUR. ACADEMIC ABOLITIONISM

1. For example, Angela Davis, *Freedom Is a Constant Struggle: Ferguson, Palestine, and the Foundations of a Movement* (Chicago: Haymarket, 2016).

2. Piya Chatterjee and Sunaina Maira, eds., *The Imperial University: Academic Repression and Scholarly Dissent* (Minneapolis: University of Min-

nesota Press, 2014); Stefano Harney and Fred Moten, *The Undercommons: Fugitive Planning and Black Study* (New York: Autonomedia, 2013).

3. Stefano Harney and Fred Moten, *The Undercommons: Fugitive Planning and Black Study* (New York: Autonomedia, 2013).

4. In our edited volume *The Imperial University: Academic Repression and Scholarly Dissent* Piya Chatterjee and I attempted to assemble an archive of stories by heretical scholars and experiences of "academic containment," including of critical knowledge about Palestine-Israel.

5. See Lisa Duggan, *The Twilight of Inequality: Neoliberalism, Cultural Politics, and the Attack on Democracy* (Boston: Beacon Press, 2003).

6. "California Scholars for Academic Freedom Lay Out History of Assaults," October 5, 2016, www.usacbi.org/2016/10/california-scholars-for-academic-freedom-lay-out-recent-history-of-assaults-on-universities-regarding-academic-freedom.

7. Steven Salaita, *Uncivil Rites: Palestine and the Limits of Academic Freedom* (Chicago: Haymarket, 2015).

8. Ibid., 31.

9. See www.change.org/p/reinstate-professor-steven-salaita.

10. Salaita sued the UIUC and ended up getting a legal settlement, in which the UIUC admitted wrongdoing; the chancellor resigned in the midst of an ethics investigation; and Freedom of Information Act requests revealed the external pressure from Zionist alumni, donors, and others to deny Salaita a job at UIUC. See www.thenation.com/article/steven-salaita-professor-fired-for-uncivil-tweets-vindicated-in-federal-court/.

11. Vicente M. Diaz, "Academic Ambush: University Gutting Indigenous Studies," June 24, 2105, *Indian Country Today,* http://indiancountrytodaymedianetwork.com/2015/06/24/academic-ambush-university-hates-indigenous-studies.

12. See Steven Salaita, *Inter/nationalism: Decolonizing Native America and Palestine* (Minneapolis: University of Minnesota Press, 2016).

13. Ibid., 137.

14. Tithi Bhattacharya and Bill V. Mullen, "Steven Salaita's Firing Shows Where Zionism Meets Neoliberalism on U.S. University

Campuses," in *Against Apartheid: The Case for Boycotting Israeli Universities*, edited by Ashley Dawson and Bill V. Mullen (Chicago: Haymarket, 2015), 201–4.

15. Ibid., 203.

16. www.usacbi.org/2015/08/ue-becomes-first-national-u-s-union-to-endorse-bds/.

17. www.usacbi.org/2014/12/historic-victory-in-us-labor-as-uaw-2865-votes-for-bds-in-landslide-resolution/.

18. www.usacbi.org/faculty-for-justice-in-palestine/.

19. Chip Gibbons, "Anti-Boycott Bills Are Part of Wider Crackdown on Protest," March 17, 2017, www.nlg.org/anti-boycott-bills-are-part-of-wider-crackdown-on-protest/.

20. Harney and Moten, *Undercommons*, 42; Julia Oparah, "Challenging Complicity: The Neoliberal University and the Prison-Industrial Complex," in Chatterjee and Maira, *Imperial University*, 116.

21. Oparah, "Challenging Complicity," 115.

22. Steven Salaita, "BDS beyond Palestine," in "The Academic Boycott Movement," edited by Sunaina Maira and Neferti Tadiar, special issue of *Social Text/Periscope*, November 2016, https://socialtextjournal.org/periscope_article/bds-beyond-palestine/.

23. Salaita, *Inter/nationalism*, 28.

24. Salaita, "BDS beyond Palestine."

25. Salaita, *Inter/nationalism*, ix.

26. Ilan Pappe, "The Boycott Will Work," in *Against Apartheid: The Case for Boycotting Israeli Universities*, edited by Ashley Dawson and Bill V. Mullen (Chicago: Haymarket, 2015), 114.

27. Ibid., 116.

28. See reports by Academic Watch, Mossawa Centre, and Right to Enter campaign at www.usacbi.org/ (go to Reports and Resources).

29. Salma Musa, "BDS and Third World Internationalism," in "The Academic Boycott Movement," edited by Sunaina Maira and Neferti Tadiar, special issue of *Social Text/Periscope*, November 2016, http://socialtextjournal.org/periscope_article/bds-and-third-world-internationalism/.

30. Ibid.

31. Kristian D. Bailey, "Strengthening Anti-Racist Politics within BDS," in "The Academic Boycott Movement," edited by Sunaina Maira and Neferti Tadiar, special issue of *Social Text/Periscope,* November 2016, https://socialtextjournal.org/periscope_article/strengthening-anti-racist-politics-within-bds/.

32. See www.blackforpalestine.com/.

33. Robin Kelley, "An Anti-Racist Movement," in "The Academic Boycott Movement," edited by Sunaina Maira and Neferti Tadiar, special issue of *Social Text/Periscope,* November 2016, https://socialtextjournal.org/periscope_article/an-anti-racist-movement/.

34. Ibid.

35. Bailey, "Strengthening Anti-Racist Politics."

36. Musa, "BDS and Third World Internationalism."

37. For example, statements by the BDS National Committee (BNC) during popular uprisings in Palestine, such as: https://bdsmovement.net/news/solidarity-palestinian-popular-resistance-boycott-israel-now.

38. Salaita, "BDS beyond Palestine."

39. www.womenstrikeus.org/our-platform/.

40. Omar Barghouti, *BDS-Boycott, Divestment, and Sanctions: The Global Struggle for Palestinian Rights* (Chicago: Haymarket, 2011) 233.

GLOSSARY

ACADEMIC FREEDOM The principle that academics have the freedom
to teach, express, and publish ideas and facts as part of the mission
of the university to promote critical discussion and independent
thought, even if that challenges the status quo, state interests, or
powerful political forces. The Declaration of Principles on
Academic Freedom and Academic Tenure, issued by the American Association of University Professors in 1915, conceptualizes
academic freedom as based on compliance with professional
norms that require professional self-regulation for academic
autonomy. Yet this view of procedural freedom for academic
workers has a complicated relationship with the ethos of political
freedom and the political environment, in which freedom of
expression is often constrained, regulated, and policed. Critical
speech about Palestine-Israel is often treated as an exception to
the right to academic freedom.

APARTHEID The 1973 International Convention on the Suppression
and Punishment of the Crime of Apartheid condemned apartheid
as entailing "inhuman acts committed for the purpose of establishing and maintaining domination by one racial group of
persons over any other racial group of persons and systematically

oppressing them." Apartheid is a system of racial control based on laws codifying a racial hierarchy of groups with different rights and privileges and, in the case of South Africa, upholding White superiority. It includes the racial segregation of the population in geographic spaces, or "bantustans," and uses security as a rationale for racialized policies of incarceration and repression. While the Israeli system of apartheid differs in some respects from South Africa's, scholars as well as South African leaders and thinkers have demonstrated how this definition is applicable to the case of Palestine.

NEOLIBERALISM An economic policy as well as cultural framework based on the deregulation of the market, privatization, and erosion of social welfare that positions citizens as consumers. Accompanying these economic measures is the notion of self-sufficiency, autonomy, and choice and the reframing of public education as a marketplace instead of a public good to which citizens have a right. The neoliberalization of the university is based on the increasing privatization of higher education as well as the notion that students, too, are consumers and the university must function as a profit-making corporation, thereby eroding its mission of producing critical thought independent of the dictates of the market.

ORIENTALISM A reference to the beliefs encoded in the field of study focused on the "Orient," as critiqued by Palestinian scholar Edward Said in his seminal book *Orientalism* (1978). European scholars since the eighteenth century viewed Asia, North Africa, and the Middle East through a set of abstractions and ahistoric generalizations based on the notion that "the West" (or Occident) and the Orient were fundamentally opposed: the West was civilized, rational, humane, and democratic, and the Orient uncivilized, backward, irrational, violent, and repressive, if exotic. This system of distinctions homogenized the diverse peoples and societies of "the East" and framed Arabs and Muslims as a threat to be contained, thus legitimizing Western colonization, as Said pointed out. He also observed that American Orientalism has been filtered through the specific U.S. relationship to the Middle East and shaped by its alliance with Israel. Knowledge produced by Orientalist "experts" is historically in the service of power and imperialism, and Orientalist notions continue to infuse dominant representations of the Middle East and Islam in the mainstream media today, particularly in discussions of Palestine-Israel as well as the BDS movement.

SETTLER COLONIALISM A form of colonialism based on extermination or expulsion of the majority of the indigenous population, who are replaced by settlers (Veracini 2013). It is a structure whose organizing principle is the "logic of elimination" (Wolfe 2006), which targets racialized populations as in the cases of the United States, Canada, and Australia. It is distinct from classic colonialism, in which indigenous populations are dominated by colonial rulers based in a metropole, or center of empire. Territory is key to settler colonial invasion and domination, and the landscape is framed as an empty land, or *terra nullius*, justifying an invasion of settlers. Settler colonialism aims to destroy indigenous sovereignty and to transform settlers into "natives" themselves, thus legitimizing their settlement and claim to the land, as in Palestine (Sayegh 1965).

WAR OF POSITION / WAR OF MANEUVER Italian Communist leader and writer Antonio Gramsci conceptualized the war of position, or cultural and intellectual struggle, in contrast to the war of maneuver, or direct war and open insurrection. The war of position is the slow, ongoing struggle over ideas and beliefs waged on the cultural front against the hegemony of the dominant class (or rule by consent of the masses) in the absence of armed struggle, but which can nonetheless lead to, or accompany, a militarized struggle and continue after it. The war of position is necessary in order to challenge dominant ideas about what is legitimate in the social order and establish a counter-hegemony. It is in this sense that the boycott movement wages a war of position.

ZIONISM The belief that Jews should establish their own homeland, modern Zionism, as led by figures such as Theodor Herzl, was a Jewish nationalist project that pivoted on the goal of creating a sovereign Jewish state in response to anti-Semitism in Europe.

However, the Zionist project that culminated in the creation of the state of Israel in 1948 in Palestine led to the mass displacement of approximately 700,000 Palestinians, who became refugees; dispossession and destruction of hundreds of Palestinian villages and towns; and violent attacks and massacres. Thus, Zionism is a settler colonialist project that is justified by exceptionalist and racist arguments rationalizing the continuing displacement of indigenous Palestinians and threats to their survival.

SELECTED BIBLIOGRAPHY

Abunimah, Ali. 2014. *The Battle for Justice in Palestine*. Chicago: Haymarket.

Barghouti, Omar. 2011. *BDS-Boycott, Divestment, and Sanctions: The Global Struggle for Palestinian Rights*. Chicago: Haymarket.

Barrows-Friedman, Nora. 2014. *In Our Power: U.S. Students Organize for Justice in Palestine*. Charlottesville, VA: Just World.

Carson, Clayborne. 1995 ed. *In Struggle: SNCC and the Black Awakening of the 1960s*. Cambridge: Harvard University Press.

Carson, Clayborne et al., eds. 1991. *The Eyes on the Prize Civil Rights Reader: Documents, Speeches, and Firsthand Accounts from the Black Freedom Struggle*. New York: Penguin.

Dawson, Ashley, and Bill V. Mullen, eds. 2015. *Against Apartheid: The Case for Boycotting Israeli Universities*. Chicago: Haymarket.

Feld, Marjorie. 2014. *Nations Divided: American Jews and the Struggle over Apartheid*. Palgrave Macmillan.

Garcia, Matt. 2012. *From the Jaws of Victory: The Triumph and Tragedy of Cesar Chavez and the Farmworker Movement*. Berkeley: University of California Press.

Marable, Manning. 2007. *Race, Reform, and Rebellion: The Second Reconstruction in Black America, 1945–2006*, 3rd ed. Jackson: University Press of Mississippi.

Qumsiyeh, Mazin. 2011. *Popular Resistance in Palestine: A History of Hope and Empowerment*. London: Pluto Press.

Salaita, Steven. 2006. *The Holy Land in Transit: Colonialism and the Quest for Canaan*. Syracuse, NY: Syracuse University Press.

———. 2015. *Uncivil Rites: Palestine and the Limits of Academic Freedom*. Chicago: Haymarket.

———. 2016. *Inter/nationalism: Decolonizing Native America and Palestine*. Minneapolis: University of Minnesota Press.

Sayegh, Fayez. 1965. *The Zionist Colonization of Palestine*. Beirut: Institute of Palestine Studies.

Veracini, Lorenzo. 2013. The Other Shift: Settler Colonialism, Israel, and the Occupation. *Journal of Palestine Studies* 42(2): 26–42.

White, Ben. 2009. *Israeli Apartheid: A Beginner's Guide*. London: Pluto Press.

Wolfe, Patrick. 2006. Settler Colonialism and the Elimination of the Native. *Journal of Genocide Research* 8(4): 387–409.